Remerciements

Many thanks to my students who taught me and allowed my tentative experimenting, to all the teachers who shared their case studies with me, and to the manuscript readers who provided valuable feedback: Alistair Caine, Manuela Cohen, Sally Cuenin, Thea Bredie, Françoise L'Eplattenier, Dee Führer, Petra Koch, Heather Murray, Margaret Niethammer, Francisco Rodriguez, Tanfele Ruoma and an unknown reader at Longman. Damien Tunnacliffe and Helena Gomm of Longman guided the manuscript through its various phases with much belief and encouragement, even allowing a few fancy flights of butterfly digression. Special thanks to Melody Noll whose copious comments and experience were the source of further clarification and a widening of perspective, and to the Baden branch of ETAS for their pioneering surveys.

I would also like to thank the authors (listed in the bibliography) who helped me to understand much of what was going on. All of life is 'work in progress', and books and ideas should be understood similarly. Any short or 'longcomings', however, are my responsibility.

Tim Murphey

N.B. 1 In the case histories, names and characteristics have been changed somewhat to safeguard the privacy of clients. The essence of the interactions however remains faithful to highlight the various learning styles and discourse strategies.

N.B. 2 In this book the pronouns used to refer to unknown persons, such as 'learner' and 'teacher', are 'she', 'hers', and 'her'. They have been chosen as a stylistic convenience and are intended as unmarked forms. They will prove to be the most useful to those people who find them the most bothersome, as a new perspective of the world is imposed. Puzzling cognitive conflict is a wonderful learning process. It's something like wearing your watch 'upside down' on purpose, after a while we learn how to read it that way and we learn that we can read everybody else's watch easier as well (since theirs appears the same as our 'upside down' watch). The use of masculine or feminine pronouns is neither right nor wrong, just as north is not down nor up, just as a watch can't be upside down. Conventionally designated 'wrong' and 'right' for these things merely shows us we have only one perspective. It's healthy, more interesting, and immensely more fun to prod ourselves into the fascinating world of multiperspectivity.

CONTENTS

■ CHAPTER 5 MATERIALS, IDEAS AND TECHNIQUES

■ CHAPTER 6 PRACTICAL CONSIDERATIONS

Preface

Genesis

This book looks at 1/1 teaching through relevant case studies and offers insights and advice for those who are involved in, or wish to begin, such teaching. The observations spring from the experience of concurrently teaching regular language classes, holding 1/1 meetings with 'classophobics', and studying applied linguistics in Switzerland. For me, there is an enormous difference between teaching individuals and groups which linguistics and teaching have helped me to understand.

I have yet to meet a teacher, with a few years' experience, who has not taught 1/1 at some time; although few do it full time. In some language schools 1/1 now accounts for a sizable portion of their business, and more and more school directors are beginning to take it seriously. Though no one has yet adequately measured the popularity of 1/1 teaching, Durban (1988) reports from a small survey of English teachers in France that 'somewhat surprisingly, 53 per cent take private students'. She wonders if this is 'the butter on the bread'. I suspect that is how most teachers see it; however, it could very well be the caviar.

With the paucity of information circulating, most teachers don't know what others are doing in 1/1 and the novice is at a loss as to how to get started. This book addresses these lacunae. Some may not even know that it is a 'field', as it has received so little attention. However, one need only look into neighbouring linguistic and psychological sciences to realise that many researchers do see 1/1 communication as the most fertile ground of language acquisition and learning. This research has inspired many teachers to make classrooms more 1/1-like (see Chapter 7).

From talking to teachers in many countries and in a variety of situations, I have found that the great majority of the 1/1 teaching is being done by teachers freelancing without the support of a school; they may very well work for a school, but usually do 1/1 teaching in their own time. Even when they do teach 1/1, in or out of a school, teachers are usually freelancing in another sense: experimenting, in that they learn how to do it as they do it, because there are few programmes, materials, and books which address 1/1 teaching specifically. Students who take 1/1 lessons are also freelancing in that first-timers are exploring a new way to learn a language and they may also feel more 'free' to launch themselves into communication without a whole class listening in. Even in regular classrooms when the 1/1 configuration is given priority in pair work, students are extremely liberated and display a much wider use of forms and functions.

So this book is also for the regular classroom teacher in each of us. Many of our observations about 1/1 can help make our classes more naturally conversational and make us realise the power in pairs, peer tutoring, and small group discussions. Teaching 1/1 can be excellent for teacher development as many of the 'inhuman' things we do to students in classes become blatant in 1/1, and we are forced to have different perspectives and to create other strategies.

This book's goal is not to be scientifically convincing, but to raise stimulating ideas from practical experience that you can come to your own conclusions about. Nevertheless, I have referred to research where it can provide evidence which may clarify intuitions. Some accepted practices will be questioned, new strategies proposed and old ideas viewed in different ways. I am not proposing any one methodology but, rather, eclectic perspectives.

Finally, and this should be first, the book is indirectly for all the potential students who would welcome and benefit from the approaches outlined in the following pages. My feeling is that the potential market of adult students who refuse to return to conventional language classes is enormous and relatively untapped.

I've tried to write this book in a one to one style. I hope it talks to you, and you with it. And I would honestly like to know your reactions and ideas, as I feel strongly that it is in interaction that we grow the most. Thus, it would be highly advisable, when possible, to read this book (or any book for that matter) with a partner, discussing chapters and your reactions as you proceed. Checking and contesting what is written against the background of two readers will render any book manifoldly more valuable, not necessarily due to what is in the book, but due more to the potentially rich interaction of the two readers.

Tim Murphey
Nanzan University
18 Yamazato-cho
Showa-ku
Nagoya 466
Japan

N.B. Chapters do not necessarily have to be read in order; you may wish to jump directly to an area of concern. Leafing through the book before reading it will also give you a better idea of its organisation and the different perspectives that it presents.

1 Introduction: 1/1 Principles

■■ This chapter introduces several ideas which help to clarify the specificity of 1/1 interaction. Most of it is down-to-earth common sense, i.e. we don't usually think about it.

Before beginning to read, consider the following questions for a moment and try to jot down a brief answer in the margin (and/or discuss them with a colleague). Doing so will help you to evaluate my thoughts in the following sections with more critical awareness.

1 How often do we speak to more than one person at a time?
2 How often do we voluntarily place ourselves in positions of weakness, that is, positions when we are the weak partner in a conversation?
3 How often do we adjust our communications to others?
4 Do we feel more involved when we only listen or when we have to talk? In which situation do we learn more?
5 What determines where we decide to sit in relation to a speaker who is talking to a group? What is the result of our relative proximity?
6 What does a good learner do to learn in a group situation?

1 Individual vs group talk

How often do we speak to more than one person at a time?

Most of the communication that we are involved in during our lives is done in pairs, or, as the title of this book suggests, '1/1'. We may often be in group settings but we usually address individuals, not the group as a whole. I have no statistics, so let me unscientifically tell you that on a normal day as a teacher, I may teach five hours and spend another one in a staff meeting in which, ostensibly, I will be addressing a group.

However, at least half of the time in my classes and meetings I notice that I am addressing one individual, not the whole group. Even at dinner with my children, I rarely have the attention of more than one child at a time. (This is no reflection on me as an authority figure but rather on my children as individuals who naturally pay more attention when addressed individually.) Those who speak regularly to groups will often admit that, even when they are 'mass communicating' at their best, they pretend that they are speaking to one person so that they can achieve a conversational tone of ease and comfort.

Let me dare to guess that approximately 90 per cent of all our oral communicating is done between only two people, one person to one person (and this applies even to teachers). Communicating with individuals, as opposed to groups, is easier, more efficient, and more comfortable for at least three reasons:

First, 'feedback attention' is focused on one person. When we are communicating with two other people, our attention is divided between the two and our efficiency of monitoring the feedback diminishes. The efficiency of our attention normally decreases proportionately to the increase in the number of people. Teachers will readily attest to the difficulty that normally accompanies larger classes as opposed to smaller ones.

Secondly, 'adjustment possibilities', our ability to adjust to attended feedback, are also normally reduced proportionately to the increase in the number of people we are expected to adjust to. Sitting with a conversation partner across a café table, we can adjust to the situation (café noises), our partner's mood (sad, happy, confused), physically (by posture and eye contact), to the level of maturity, and interest topics. Trying to adjust on all these levels to even one person demands intense awareness and flexibility. Multiply these levels by more individuals and the task becomes that much more difficult.

Thirdly, 'affective inhibition', or emotional energy, that may cause reluctance to participate, may also increase with the number of people involved in the communication. Teachers are very familiar with students who seem to be endlessly talking to their friends during class but who clam up when asked to speak to the group.

2 Unequal encounters
How often do we voluntarily place ourselves in positions of weakness?

One of the most inhibiting factors in learning or improving a language is the 'unknowing' which places the student in the 'weak' position and the teacher in the 'strong'. This is presumably one of the main reasons that executives and others who are normally in strong roles in business and industry are extremely reluctant to return to schools in which, traditionally, students are in a weak position. This is also why they are willing to pay high prices to a tutor, without the inhibiting presence of lesser gods who may outperform them and will certainly take some of the teacher's attention away from them. The study of 'unequal encounters' (see Thomas, 1984), and the inhibiting discourse strategies involved, is a new field, but there is already sufficient evidence to see the advantages of adjusting teacher behaviour toward 'equal encounters', or toward a balance of power. The basic equalising ingredient is respect. This equalising of the partners does not imply a lack of leadership on the part of the teacher. Most students will want both respect and 'guided push' from a teacher. While they want a teacher to give direction and to motivate, they also will learn more, and more willingly, if the teacher adapts to their interests, learning styles, etc. and shows clear respect for the person. The process of doing so will be illustrated in the case histories in Chapter 2 and discussed in the conclusion.

3 Adjusting to others
How often do we adjust our communication to others?

Adjustment is a basic principle in many domains. In Darwin's explanation of the survival of a species it is referred to as 'adaptation'. We adjust or adapt to survive. In business and economics it is called responding to supply and demand. History is rife with examples of those who adjusted to change and those who didn't. Efficiently adjusting to the messages we receive, and appropriately adjusting those that we send, are strategies basic to survival, longevity, and success in each of these domains.

Sociolinguistically, we adjust differently to children, those outside our profession, and other adults of different socio-cultural strata. But even inside one group we make minor adjustments to the individuals and we dynamically adjust as we monitor their reception and feedback.

Adjustment is a big word in 1/1 encounters. The possibility for greater individual adjustment in 1/1 is probably its main advantage. Trying to adjust to a class of twenty different personalities, interest topics, and momentary emotional fluctuations, and at the same time physically giving eye contact and attending to body language, is practically impossible. A teacher in this situation may become a 'mass media feeder'. When circulating and adjusting individually to each student, she even then only gives a few minutes to each and may have to go through enormous changes in order to tune in appropriately.

Dick Allwright (at the 1988 TESOL France Conference) tells an anecdote about his thirteen-year-old daughter who noticed a difference in her inexperienced teacher's questions and answers when addressed to the group and to her individually. The questions apparently got little response when addressed to the group, but circulating, the teacher seemed to change his questioning strategies and she was more willing to try to answer. Also his answers to questions from the group were rather evasive and defensive, while 1/1 he became friendlier and took more care in answering. Allwright's daughter also mentioned that she sometimes asked questions because she thought her teacher needed one at the time, apparently needing to interact instead of just act upon others. It seems, just speaking without sincerely soliciting collaboration is not a very natural way to speak to people in any case and quite difficult for beginning teachers. Perversely, it takes years of hard training to be comfortable ignoring your audience and just talking at them.

This is not to say that classroom teaching should be done away with. Mass media and group discourse do have their advantages. However the major thesis here is that **to a great extent language learning, or for that matter any learning, is more efficient where the participating parties can adjust maximally to each other.**

Adjustment in language learning behaviour has become recognised as a great creator of comprehensible input and an acquisition facilitator.

4 Involvement

Do we feel more involved when we have only to listen or when we present? In which situation do we learn more usually?

Involvement is another big word. 1/1 implies that two people are involved in interaction. It's easy to be uninvolved in large classroom situations, nearly impossible when someone is talking to you alone. Thus, our difficulty in getting rid of door-to-door salesmen and evangelists. When you do impolitely close the door in their faces, you feel bad because you've broken the involvement rule of discourse and you haven't allowed the script to run its course (opening, information exchange, closing). Or you do let it run its course and feel bad for spending an hour at the door because they have refused to close the discourse. People are hard to ignore 1/1, and some abuse this fact.

It is also hard to be uninvolved when you are conveying your own knowledge, which is the reason why teachers are potentially the greatest learners and why students can often learn more when encouraged to teach their classmates and share their information and ideas (discussed in more detail in Chapter 7).

5 Proximity

What determines where we sit in proximity to a speaker who is addressing a group and what effect does our choice have?

Ski analogy 1

Of course, the 1/1 principle of maximally adjusted communication for learning has further application beyond language teaching. From the bird's-eye view of a ski lift, watch any ski school class winding its way down a slope behind its teacher like a snake – albeit disjointed at times. If you watch closely and for long enough you'll usually find that the student who is just behind the instructor does a much better job of imitating and following her path.

The other students skiing further back seem to wander and to be vaguely following but, because of the lack of proximity, the teacher has trouble communicating with them and receiving their feedback, i.e. monitoring their physical adjustments to her instructions. Of course ski teachers are aware of this and rotate the position of the students so that each can get more individual attention at some time during the lesson.

In a language lesson, if a teacher gives a sixty minute lesson to even ten students, she can only be intensely communicating, that is, giving total attention to the 'feedback-adjusting-circuit', with each student six minutes every lesson. The rest of the time, students are in reasonably uninvolved, low-risk situations in that they are not being personally addressed, or, if they are, it is as that vague entity called the 'group' (unless pair and small group work is used, see Chapter 7). Contrastingly, students taking 1/1 instruction may become quickly tired and frustrated if teachers teach in a conventionally class-intensive way and see correction and information giving as their major role. This isn't to say that 1/1 cannot be intensive, rather that it is intensive in a different way, hopefully a more relaxing and humanly interpersonal way.

6 Learning in groups
What does a good learner do to learn in a group situation?

Learning from group discourse and observing 1/1

To be fair, we must admit that the preceding paragraphs are somewhat misleading in that learning and acquisition can and do occur without total individual attention. Indeed, the efficient learner in group situations learns to take group discourse and interpret it individually for her needs. She also learns from monitoring her peers, noticing (often subconsciously) what they do well and what they seem to be doing wrong, and possibly from forming hypotheses on the processes.

Also, it could very well be that a learner when in a mode of quality observation can observe a 1/1 pair in which the parties adjust well to each other, and through such observation acquire information, language, and adjustment strategies. However, for this to happen several criteria need to be met. The observer must be 'on' (i.e. attentive to what's going on), 'ready' for acquiring such information (i.e. it is at her approximate level), and of course the observed parties must produce quality adjustments that transparently lead to some identifiable outcome. The fact is that we are not always attentive to such things and I would suggest that while observation of others is a useful learning mechanism, more intensive learning takes place with involvement. The critical factor in involvement seems to be how good at adjusting to and stimulating each other the partners are.

There are also group communications that are relevant to one and all. However, the intensity of relevancy may vary greatly among the individuals in any one group, considering the diversity of interests, each person's background knowledge and experience through which they interpret information, and their changing emotions. These group communications also usually require a particular medium as well (e.g. radio, T.V., microphone) and a gifted communicator. One of the appealing things about T.V. may be that it seems to focus its attention on the spectator like a hypnotising madonna (a good eye contact one to one person), thus its usefulness in some parents' eyes as a babysitter, and its abuse in the eyes of social ecologists who refer to whole apathetic populations as being 'babysat upon'.

Mass production is often an efficient process in industry. I think it rarely is in language acquisition. Humans communicate and learn most efficiently with individualised attention, i.e. adjusted to each of their individual selves.

The energy of this book springs from the conviction that communication is most successfully done 1/1, that is, individuals talking to individuals, adjusting to each other linguistically, emotionally and topically, individuals learning from each other interpersonally. Successful language learning is mostly done in the same way, either in teacher–student pairs, student–student pairs, or simply with friends in natural interaction.

2 Case histories

This chapter takes you through a variety of case histories. Probably the most important thing to learn from them is that we have so much to learn from our students.

During my second year of graduate studies in Switzerland, while waiting for an assistant's post that I would have the following year, I quit my teaching job in a local private school to concentrate on my books. However, finding books hard to digest with my stomach growling, I decided to give a few private lessons a week. That is, if I could find them. I put fifty-three announcements up on school and community bulletin boards. They looked something like this:

English Lessons

INTERESTING AND FUN
Native Speaker

Contact: (my name and address)

Needless to say, I was no blossoming publicity genius, and as I was without a telephone, my announcement was tantamount to saying 'don't contact me'. The advertisement received no response for six weeks, and then only one. In the meantime, I gave lessons to my downstairs neighbour, Ariane, who was in evening classes trying to get her high school baccalaureate.

Case 1: Ariane – 6 months

I don't know if Ariane ever passed her 'bac', but she passed me on to a friend of hers who was taking the same course, and her husband put me in touch with a banker friend who wanted lessons, who put me in touch with his brother-in-law, and so on, until I had ten students a week after three months.

■ Observation 1

Your students are your best publicity. Let them know you are looking for other students and the connections multiply. Advertising may be necessary to get the word out, but personal contacts will ultimately bring in more business. Such referrals are also much more reliable in that referred students are usually friendlier and take less effort adjusting to because they know a little about you and what to expect through another student.

Ariane was a 33-year-old housewife with four children who was determined to finish her 'bac' of which English was one of the chosen subjects. We held classes in her kitchen and concentrated on the books that she was supposed to read, and about which she would be questioned at her oral exams (works by Maugham, Steinbeck and Hemingway).

Ariane turned out to be a 'monitor maniac' (Krashen, 1981) in that she concentrated so much on pronunciation and grammar that she had difficulty carrying on a conversation. She also had a very exact idea of how the lessons should be because she had learned German in school fifteen years previously. Our first lessons contained a lot of student-solicited grammatical explanations and pronunciation correction. She often asked 'Why do you say it that way? What's the rule?' She wanted things written down and then put into the past tense. She would stop in mid sentence to ask if what she had said so far was correct, and then forget what she was going to say in the first place. Sometimes she looked disappointedly at me and accused me of not correcting her enough, as her teachers had always done in school. So I would interrupt her more, and she would masochistically thank me.

Ariane's high amount of nervous stress, or 'affective filter' (Ibid.), was also a problem. She would begin each session with her books piled high on the table saying she only had six months. Before actually beginning she would tell me, in French, about the great amount of work to do in the other classes and the various domestic concerns that were preoccupying her at the moment. Under such stress, relaxing was difficult. Still, to talk about the problems for a few minutes before working seemed to calm her down. Then we would begin work, which unfortunately was devoid of the intense communicating which she had just finished doing in French.

As she was my first private student, I wanted to try to adjust to her needs and desires and let her direct the learning. If she wanted to learn every tense and stress for each two-word verb, I was there to tense and stress her. However, after a few sessions with Ariane, I became frustrated with the slow progress and tried to explain in non abstract language that for ease of communication she perhaps needed to listen a lot at first and then to speak, that every error need not be corrected, that we should try for a bit of fluency instead of pure accuracy devoid of meaning.

I also tried to persuade her that we needed to talk about real things at first because the books were too artificial and too advanced for her level. (She had translated entire pages in pencil above each line, confessing to having looked every fifth word up in the dictionary – a sure way not to enjoy literature!) She agreed and for a few lessons we had our preliminary settling down discussions in English instead of French, with me guessing meaning and translating immediately when she slipped into French.

To calm her stress over the books, I read them and recorded myself giving a summary on cassette. She listened to the cassettes during the day while doing other tasks and in later lessons we discussed the different story lines and interpretations, although in a very elementary fashion. Later still, I gave her possible test questions concerning the works that she prepared first in writing and then presented orally, being corrected by me at each stage.

Ariane never totally got over her monitor mania, although she did make some progress. In the end, her courageous determination inhibited her ability to follow more natural language learning strategies. The artificial language learning goal, i.e. passing her exams, was also unnaturally high for her level. Like a beginning high-jumper who puts the bar at a high competitive level instead of training at a reasonable height and then progressing, Ariane became inevitably frustrated no matter how fixed her will.

In addition to the artificial goal, our situation was also somewhat artificial, that is, her teacher was not the best possible choice. She had been speaking French with me for a few months before beginning lessons and it was the comfortable natural means of communication. The knowledge that French was the easiest way to communicate affected us adversely when we struggled in English. It was an uncomfortable game for us both. Further difficulties may have been due to the redefining of roles, i.e. from friend to teacher. Later we will see that these roles can coexist, but that it is preferable to begin as teacher. My sceptical side wonders whether it is wise to even take friends and acquaintances as students. And yet, as with everything else, it probably depends on the individuals involved.

▬ Observation 2
If possible, make English the only language of communication from the very beginning and it becomes the accepted standard. Even if the student becomes aware of the teacher's ability to converse in the student's language, it remains a secondary resource that can be seen as enhancing the situation when needed, but not dominating it.

Case 2: Maria – 6 months

Maria was a 38-year-old mother of two who was also going to evening classes for her 'bac'. Meeting her for the first time, English was established as the basis of our interaction instead of French. Maria was of Spanish origin and as a child immigrant learned French. Because of this background she was more open to natural language learning than was Ariane and seemed to progress greatly over a six-month period.

Lessons were in her kitchen over a good cup of coffee which created a kind of intimate café, just relaxed enough without distractions. Her two adolescent boys were also taking English in school and were very much interested in English pop music. Our warm-up discussions usually centred around her coffee and her family.

Maria also showed the Latin talent of interpreting most things personally while working with the books she had chosen for her exams. How the works related to her family and life were her natural concern. With new expressions that we came across, she immediately tried to use them in talking about her sons or husband.

■ Observation 3

The efficient learner has the practised ability to change mass media discourse into personally relevant communication, to imagine that the speaker or writer is addressing her. Interestingly enough, part of the appeal of pop songs, advertising, and even fairy tales lies in the fact that they are usually not tied to specific times, places, and people, with the result that their discourse is easily appropriated by the receiver for personal use. (See Bronckart (1987) on disjointed and conjointed discourse, Rotzoll (1985) on advertisements, Bornoz (1988) on fairy tales, and Murphey (1989, 1990b) on pop songs.) To a certain extent the teacher can aid this process by asking student-centred questions concerning ideas and topics, i.e. by presenting a framework of language which the students fill in with content from their lives. (See 'Insearch' – Appendix 8.)

Maria willingly went through a listening stage with me where she said very little but showed comprehension by body language, agreement and following sounds, eye contact and actions. Later our discussions simulated her oral exams. Although her level of English was not much greater than Ariane's at the beginning, she was soon having lengthy and meaningful discussions with me.

Another feature that helped was the interest that she was showing in her sons' studies and interest in pop music. For her, English was somewhat *instrumental* in that it put her in touch with her children more since pop music and their English classes became common subjects of discussion.

■ Observation 4

Having *instrumental* motivation means learning things that one sees as useful for life, and it not only makes learning more interesting but more efficient. With learning that is merely *incidental*, the goals are generally getting on with things and getting good grades, not actually *using* the language. A third kind of motivation, and the most efficient in some people's opinion, is *integrative*, in which the student identifies with the group, or wants to become part of the group, that speaks the language. (See Gardner and Lambert, 1972.)

Case 3: Ben – 8 months

Ben was my first 'café class student'. A bank employee, he was hesitant as to whether he wanted lessons at first, so I agreed to meet him for a coffee and discuss it. It subsequently became routine for me to suggest to potential clients that we meet for coffee and discuss the possibility of lessons, with no obligations. This allowed students to look at the situation (and at me) with no commitment. They could always gently back out saying that they were interested but extremely busy at the moment and that they would contact me when things slowed down. This never happened, but I think it was psychologically comforting for them to have more control in the situation and start us off on an 'equal encounter'.

▬ Observation 5
Agreeing (or suggesting) to meet with no obligation to discuss possible lessons gives more control to the student. Clients may be more apt to consider teachers who don't give them a hard sell. It's a start of equal encounters. On the other hand, some teachers might argue that time is money and therefore choose to charge even for the first meeting, of course stressing that continuing is up to the student. This automatically excludes the half-serious and falsely curious, but perhaps also some potentially excellent contacts.

The first time I met Ben, we spoke French for the first fifteen minutes (thus violating Observation 2 – nothing is sacred!) and he explained why he wanted to improve his English: to handle foreign clients better at the bank and on the telephone. I listened mostly and asked questions about his job (that I later asked in English). Since both of our schedules were busy we decided to schedule meetings from one time to the next. This I found also was a reassuring policy, for he could discontinue at any time he wished, another point of control for him.

▬ Observation 6
The flexibility of the teacher is of great importance as regards meeting place and time. Although scheduling from one time to another may give little job security, some clients live with a constantly changing agenda instead of a fixed schedule and will appreciate the opportunity that a flexible teacher may offer. Others, however, may prefer the school-like security of fixed times and days.

After the first fifteen minutes, I switched to English and asked Ben about himself and his family (an easy subject) allowing him to switch back into French if he liked, not forcing it. He followed willingly and showed his determination to try in English. I didn't correct any errors and simply confirmed that I understood what he was saying, expressing interest. He was reassured and pleased that he could communicate in English. We parted, shaking hands warmly, and agreed to speak only English at the next meeting.

Our meetings were always in cafés, usually at the end of his work day. The informal atmosphere lent itself well to conversation and the closeness, across a café table, provided an intimacy that was comfortable. For many students the silence of a classroom may be uncomfortable or inhibiting and the pauses between speaking may seem to last forever. However, in the typical European environment of the café, there is always a social background noise which seems to stimulate even the shyest to get out of their shell.

Although other teachers may raise their eyebrows and ask how one could possibly teach in a noisy hotel lobby or coffee shop, showing them your full agenda usually puts them in a reflective mood. Still, there is the risk that clients might think that they are just paying for talk. No matter how convinced their teacher is that 'talk' is an excellent way for them to improve, the students still have experience as students and need something more concrete to justify their paying for lessons.

This psychological need for some sort of 'schoolishness' can be provided by notes and auxiliary materials. With Ben I developed a note-taking technique in which I jotted down, as inconspicuously as possible, errors, idioms and vocabulary options, pronunciation problems, grammatical notes, and ideas during the first fifty minutes of our meeting. We spent the last ten minutes going over my notes. At the end he left with the notes in his briefcase as a sort of record of what went on. This corresponded with school notes and could be studied at home in order not to make the same errors again. Whether students actually did review them or not was not the important thing; it was rather the satisfaction of having a record, and of calming that school-conditioned animal inside them that cried out for seriousness and pain in learning.

■ Observation 7

Often the clients still need something to make them feel your meetings are somewhat like school. Even if they are progressing a lot, the enjoyment and naturalness may make them doubt the efficiency of the method because they learned in school that studying is supposed to be more difficult. This need of some sort of concrete 'schoolishness' (such as looking at the teacher's notes the last ten minutes of an hour) may be intensified by the equalising of the encounter and the non-school environment. Basically, it is a clash between different ways of looking at learning, and until the client, and perhaps the teacher, can accept learning in an unconventional way, some emphasis should be placed on conventional tools which can help them to adjust.

■ Observation 8

The pain of error correction can, however, be avoided, e.g. by taking notes and only interrupting if the communication breaks down (i.e. you don't understand). Note taking doesn't have to interrupt the flow of conversation except when immediately relevant. Ostensibly it appears to passers by that I am the student taking notes, or a journalist interviewing someone. By avoiding any blatant 'teacher-talk', someone listening in would take me for an extremely interested friend and a good listener who always has another question waiting.

It became apparent that Ben was really as interested in talking about his passion, sailing, as his profession. I was ignorant in both domains so he had to give a lot of elementary explanations. It was evident to me that he was really teaching me things about which I had very little knowledge, and using English as a medium. Concerning banking, he was explaining the same things to me that he had to explain to his clients, with the only difference being that I presented no risk and was in the role of easing and aiding his communication. The nice thing was that very often he forgot that he was speaking English, which later improved his self-confidence immensely.

■ Observation 9
When the teacher generates an intense and genuine interest in the client and the client's interests, feeling sincerely that the client has as much to teach as to learn, the creation of an *equal encounter* situation is easier.

Occasionally I gave Ben articles in English on sailing and economics suggesting that he could explain them to me at the next class. Sometimes he did, sometimes he didn't. It was not my role to demand homework; we were more colleagues and I did not want to add any unwanted stress. In any case I always had ample discussion topics so that we never ran out of things to say. Uncomfortable silences, which provoke insecurity and loss of confidence, were avoided by my having so many questions to ask. If I didn't have one stemming from his last comment, I merely went to my prepared student ego centred list (see Chapter 5.10). Or I could give him my list of questions to ask me!

With Ben I also became more conscious of tuning in to his mood and flowing with his desired discussion topics. Since he was not studying for an exam, but merely wanted to improve his conversational English to handle clients better, all subjects were good. All his clients had families and were probably in the sailboat class. So if he wanted to talk about his hard day at the office, his children going to ski camps, his sailing weekend, or the new federal tax exemption law, I was willing.

■ Observation 10
A teacher may plan extensively and have a stock of topics to discuss and materials to exploit, but does not need to feel tied to them. By tuning into the students and realising what they want to talk about at any given time and then flowing with them in the same direction, instead of causing a headwind, the teacher is participating in and aiding the learning process more than directing it. It is what we normally do anyway in unplanned meetings. It's more natural and it makes for smoother sailing.

Ben and I met once a week for a period of eight months, sometimes skipping several weeks because of commitments. For his summer vacation he asked me what I thought of his spending two weeks at a school in England. I advised him (another part of the expanding role) to go to a port city and to engage in two types of research: one in banks and one with sailboats. In banks he could go and interview the people in positions similar to his and determine the similarities and differences in procedures and then file a report with his bank (who would be paying for his studies anyway and would appreciate a concrete spinoff). Secondly, remembering how I had learned the majority of my French playing tennis and basketball, I suggested that he take an advanced sailing class. Because Ben was an excellent sailor, the messages would be familiar while much of the vocabulary would be new. Through the comradeship involved in sports he would be more in touch socially with native speakers.

To go to a language school with his intermediate level of English would not necessarily be bad, but he would run the risk of then being with other foreigners and not becoming involved enough with the natives and practising speaking with them. Whereas academic language learning may be more useful for college students who must pass exams, it is not necessarily ideal for intermediate students wanting practice in actual use.

It seemed to me that if his knowledge of banking and sailing were what brought about the possibility of an equal encounter in our meetings, then they could also enhance his meetings in England. If Swiss banks were the best in the world and had little to learn from the British banks, it didn't matter. In that case, the employees from British banks would most probably be very eager to talk to a Swiss banker and learn how he worked. And if he approached them from the aspect of humbly wanting to learn from them, the chances are they would be flattered.

■ Observation 11
The private teacher can become a valuable language acquisition consultant, advising the student first on ways to improve and speed up language learning, and secondly on ways to shape the language learning environment for increased contact time. In the first instance, it may mean showing students how to use new words in a personal context, or letting them know that studying four times a day for a quarter of an hour each is usually more profitable than one hour straight. In the second, it may mean advising them on English radio and T.V. programmes, reading material in their field, language exchange programmes, plays and presentations, and on how to get the most out of a stay abroad.

■ Observation 12
In order to attain an approximate level of 'equal encounter' a student learning a language can offer something of value to her partners. Native speakers will not communicate for long purely out of goodness, something else must be put into the bargain. This may be learning something new, a dating interest, money, etc. Language teachers get paid for adjusting, but this does not alleviate the affective problems inherent in 'unknowing' and 'unequal encounters'. Finding the student's strong points and using those as material can equalise the imbalance and give the student confidence in another domain when she is feeling inadequate with the language.

Case 4: René – 8 months

René was Ben's cousin and also a bank employee, but in a different bank. Although I was far from being monetarily endowed (and still am), he enjoyed counselling me on what to do with my imaginary millions and the different possibilities that existed.

René was my first lesson-over-lunch client, and usually nobly picked up the bill in addition to paying my fee. And since it was usually a businessman's restaurant, I adjusted and even wore the one tie I owned. Eating added another dimension to note-taking and I occasionally had to write around gravy stains.

Many of the things that I was learning with Ben at the same time, I could use with René. However, their learning styles were quite different. René loved to talk and dreamed of going to America. He disliked my note-taking and gave me the feeling that it was my psychological need that I was fulfilling, not his. And maybe it was. He truly only wanted a pleasant lunch with conversation in English. So I gradually ignored the note-taking until finally I only brought out paper to take notes for myself on investment opportunities (in case I ever got the money).

René once invited me to the bank for a lesson and proudly gave me a tour all in English like a regular client, which the other employees thought I was. Then we retired to one of the conference rooms for our lesson. With René I was able to make a list of typical things that he wanted to say to clients. He also provided me with the psychological profiles of his different clients and explained how he judged which investments were best for them. (Apparently it's not the amount of money or the quality of the investment as much as the personality of the client that must be considered when suggesting investments; that is, he adjusted to each client – sound familiar?)

■ Observation 13

Part of a teacher's adjusting seems to be figuring out to what extent the student wants lessons resembling school or simply social contact. The tenet of conventional education is that school is most efficient, but experience does not always show this to be true. Nevertheless most students are convinced that the way they learned in school is the best way, perhaps because that is the only conscious learning model they have been exposed to, but also by the sheer weight of the institution's acknowledged, if not actual, authority in such matters. Students may hate a particular learning technique but nevertheless want it and expect it because that is what they have been conditioned to understand as 'learning'. In order not to shock them and unduly excite anxiety, the teacher may at first have to teach to the learner's expectations, at least to some degree. It seems that individual students do learn more if they're convinced they are doing what they think is best, they are in control, and they are enjoying it (these are not necessarily mutually compatible criteria). But part of teaching entails showing students the different possible ways one can learn as well. As teachers we don't simply decide that this student is conventional and another more liberal and then teach accordingly. We can show each student different possibilities for learning so they then have a choice. The students' acquisition of learning strategies is a developing, dynamic process. Where they are at any one point will determine what you do during lessons.

Case 5: Carole and Karl – 8 months

Karl, an engineer friend of René's, wanted to have lessons with his wife, Carole, a secretary. In their late thirties, they were both low intermediate speakers but their reading level was much higher. We met in their apartment once a week and the difficulty of trying to keep *two* students intensely involved was immediately apparent.

Carole, being more lively and talkative, was easy to engage so that most of my conscious attention centred on how to get the more reticent Karl to interact with us. But I had to be careful not to make him uncomfortable by forever addressing my questions and comments to him. It appeared to me that he was actually more content in the spectator role. Later when he took me on a tour of his workplace, I found his lack of involvement merely part of his personality, not a reaction to being intimidated by his more fluent wife.

Thus I had two students meeting me at the same time, each with rather different learning styles and interests. My goal was to keep them both involved, so I tried to discuss what they did together without committing any intercultural *faux pas*. After exploiting the photo albums of their trips and summer vacations, I was getting hard pressed to find material suitable for them both. Thus I started bringing in communicative game material from my regular EFL classes. But I was dissatisfied that I couldn't centre an hour's conversation simply around the lives of two individuals and that when tuning in intensely to one I ran the risk of losing the other. Facing even two students reduced the amount of attention I could give to either one. The attention was also poorer quality, lacking a certain coherence and cohesiveness, since I was continually shifting from one to the other in a discontinuous attempt to involve them more.

However, I was far from being dissatisfied with their progress. My disappointment was in the realisation that I could not communicate with them as intensely as I could with a single student and make the proportionally greater amount of progress. Another possibility, that a colleague brought to my attention, might have been that I had given myself too central a role and that I should have developed more lessons in which they were interacting and I was in the background, perhaps taking notes.

■ Observation 14
The language teacher in a classroom may dominate too much when always proceeding in a lecture fashion, rather than stimulating the students to interact and use the language while the teacher is in the background. With two students, it may be that encouraging them to

interact will also help the teacher to get out of the way. But this again brings us back to a classroom situation and is no longer 1/1 with an efficiently adjusting teacher. Of course this assumes that the teacher is better than a non-native conversation partner which may not always be the case (see Varonis and Gass, 1985).

Case 6: Vincent and Pierre – 3 months

Word spread of my English lessons from the engineering department to the sales department of the same engineering firm, and I was requested to give conversation lessons to two salesmen. We met for only two months before the summer break, always for an hour a week, in the morning at their offices. Vincent was the coordinator for sales and Pierre was in charge of the German market.

Vincent felt uncomfortable being in a schoolish situation again and laughed a lot as a salesman might when he is not used to being on the other end of the sales pitch. Vincent was, to an extent, Pierre's superior, thus a type of unequal encounter was evident between the students. Pierre seemed reluctant to speak up and gave Vincent all the floor he wanted.

Although we tried to relax and have a coffee, I found once again that I was talking to two individuals who performed different tasks and had different motivations for improving their English. Vincent had clients who called him on the phone. He also had a lot of reading to do in English, whereas Pierre needed to use his English on the road, face to face with clients in Germany.

Many French speakers, although perhaps having learned German for many years in school, prefer to speak English when doing business with German speakers. Speaking a language that is foreign to both parties may be a means of creating a more 'equal encounter' situation since neither can rely on their native language and they may each approach the exchange with more humility; both must forfeit native comfort.

■■ **Observation 15**
Using a language internationally between non-natives may have an equal encounter effect that is healthy. Neither participant has the advantage of merely speaking their native language, but, rather, both must adjust with humility and pay more attention to their partner.

Case 7: Thomas and Jean – 2 months

Thomas was a semi-professional soccer player who worked part time in the telex department of a large firm and did most of his sending and receiving in English. He wanted to improve his English to do his job better, but we ended up speaking mostly about sports and girls which were his principal preoccupations, if not occupations.

Thomas was referred to me by another student, Jean, a bank employee, who would take his hour right after Thomas in the same café and was very much interested in the same topics. It was springtime and the sidewalk cafés were full of fascinating women that we could refer to. Often Thomas would linger for another drink as Jean settled in and we discussed what we would say to someone we found attractive without imposing ourselves. They were seriously motivated to discuss meeting women in English. Clichés, openers, retreats, excusing and questioning were all part of the linguistic agenda that we were exploring.

■■ Observation 16

Adjusting to your student's enthusiasm and interests may necessitate a readjustment of your own priorities at a given moment in your life, or at least an acceptance of their interests without derogatory judgement. This is especially true with adolescent learners. It helps to change your sense of humour, point of view, and mental framework in order to be more acceptable, or at least tolerable.

Rivers said it best:

As language teachers we are the most fortunate of teachers – all subjects are ours. Whatever the . . . [students] want to communicate about, whatever they want to read about, is our subject matter. The essence of language teaching is providing conditions for language learning. (1976:105)

With the interests of these two students noted, diagrammed and described, my note pad was actually more full, and certainly more studied afterwards, than it was with my other clients. With such enthusiastic students, I felt I could teach them well as long as I tuned in to their interests and motivations.

My biology teacher in high school did much the same thing when he had a class full of football players. He got us interested in our biologically functioning bodies by describing what happened to us on the football field when we ran fifty yards for a touchdown. He intrigued us further with his description of the associative pleasure that the cheerleaders felt on the sidelines. Of course not all motivation stems from our dating and hunting instincts, but if it is a manifested energy in our students, I feel it should be used, although not abused.

Case 8: Mlle Flandres – 4 years

Mlle Flandres was the only person who ever responded to the announcement that I hung on fifty-three bulletin boards. But I would put up 200 announcements every year, if I were sure to get just one more student like her.

She responded to my announcement with a three page letter – it was her way of having me adjust to her. And after five years I am still meeting with her.

In her sixties, a retired sales executive in a large firm, Mlle Flandres is a well-travelled and well-read stick of dynamite. She speaks four languages fluently (including English) and is also learning Russian. A diligent student who embraces new words, idioms, and ideas as fast as they appear, she is nevertheless interested in what I would call 'maintenance', keeping up her English. She is a teacher's ideal student.

■ Observation 17

Although the traditionally professed goal for language teachers is student progress, for certain students at certain levels, maintenance and 'keeping the batteries charged' may be their primary reason for taking lessons. Social contact may be primary for still others. However, learning new things is still very much a part of the process, for the 'recharging' is best done when going somewhere, and social contact most interesting when doing challenging things with the language. The emphasis here is principally on using and keeping useful the muscles that are already there. It may be difficult to get to the heart of the reason why someone wants lessons. To overt questions they may tell you they want it for their business. However, through the use of materials the teacher may come to find that they show little interest in 'business' things, but are more interested in other areas, and that perhaps they are not so interested in learning new vocabulary as in practising that which they already have, to activate it into fluency. The capacity of a teacher to adapt to these insights is what can make 1/1 an extremely efficient teaching situation. Again a needs and information questionnaire (see page 59) can help a lot in determining what a student wants, but these may be just surface desires. And, of course, needs and desires change as a course progresses.

Mlle Flandres and I usually meet in her living room, although occasionally for dinner or in one of Neuchâtel's cosy cafés. Inevitably, she has prepared her lesson beforehand and when I arrive, she has books, articles and paraphernalia piled high on the table with an orderly list on the top. Although I prepare things to talk to her about, we rarely get to them. She is a student who has followed, more than the others, the self-directing lesson plan where she controls the class, as I imagine she controlled board meetings before retiring.

Time flies when I am with her, and the ideas richly intertwine themselves with our language play. Sometimes we drink coffee or tea, sometimes wine or vodka (after she's come from a Russian lesson), and for special occasions champagne. We meet once or twice a week. We write a lot to each other as well. She will send me linguistic articles that she has come across concerning my studies and I will send her notes and clippings concerning the smorgasbord of ideas brought up in our discussions.

■ Observation 18

Corresponding with students and sending them cards, notes, and articles relevant to their interests is very positive and good

publicity. Not only do they feel that the teacher's concern for them goes beyond the hour lesson (which it should), but they in turn are on the lookout for the teacher's good too: sending articles of interest and more students. Correspondence is another element adding to the equal encounter.

Case 9: Mr Adler – 3 years

I am also still seeing Mr Adler at this time (after three years as I write) and we enjoy a 'maintenance' English relationship as well. Mr Adler reached me through a university professor friend of his. In his late seventies, he is a retired but extremely active historian who writes and lectures widely. I meet him for dinner once or twice a month as our busy schedules permit, always at his favourite table in a lakeside restaurant. I have also done a few translations for him for his various public and academic presentations.

I followed my usual note-taking technique at first but, like René, he wasn't interested in schoolishness. When I tried going over the notes at the end of the first few lessons, he answered politely, 'Yes, I see,' when I could see quite well they would find the rubbish bin before they got home. The pure practice and reminder that he could get his message across were his joy and reward.

▰ Observation 19

Perhaps the single greatest service that I provide to many executives is simply one of added *confidence* that they can express themselves, that they can get their messages across, that they need have no feelings of inadequacy when attempting to express themselves. I am providing a 'sheltered' situation where they can risk themselves with limited liability – I am not really a customer. I am also an encouraging listener and avid questioner so that their concentration is more on the message than the form.

An aside

In 1985 I saw an interesting exercise done with a zero-level English speaker in a workshop by Tony Stockwell that drove the above point home to me. There were many other participants who spoke varying degrees of English, but a beginner was chosen to read a five sentence paragraph out loud to the group. He obviously didn't want to at first and had little understanding as he stumbled his way through the first out-loud reading.

At the end, Stockwell said, 'That was super!' and applauded, having everyone else applaud with him. Then he asked for a second reading from the same man. It was amazing! The second reading was at least 30 per cent better with no actual instruction, only positive feedback. The man's reading fluency and intonation improved immensely simply because we provided confidence. At the end of the second reading, Stockwell again expressed great approval and we all applauded. Then the man was begged to read once more. I thought it had gone far enough, but my ears were not deceived: once again he made noticeable progress in the reading. I was nearly convinced he knew what he was saying, and maybe he did. Confidence does improve performance.

Teachers very often focus and comment on what is wrong rather than what is right. I often find myself silently marvelling at how well a student is doing and forget to share the news because I am so taken up with the message. We need to remember to praise them, too, which of course builds confidence which is so important for fluency. However, meaningless and exaggerated praise can kill the sincerity of the exchange. Praising also is pronouncing judgement. When the teacher praises with abandon the student may ask herself if she is doing something wrong when there is no praise. Let praise be a feeling, not a judgement.

Mr Adler was an unpretentious oral/aural genius and neither needed nor wanted written records. Despite all intents and purposes, I was getting a private history course adjusted to my level by an outstanding authority and he was buying me dinner and paying my fee for it. I felt guilty, sometimes.

Nevertheless, the one time I didn't bother to pull out paper and pen I had the impression that things didn't go as well as they could have – I had the impression that perhaps the paper still did add credibility to the session even though it was disliked.

Another contribution to the schoolishness were the articles in English that I brought him. I also lent him the book *Megatrends* by J. Naisbitt which gave us many points of departure for lively discussions as he related what he thought the contemporary trends and historical developments in Switzerland and Europe had been since World War II. Mr Adler remains one of my most fascinating clients.

10 Teachers as students
Exchanging roles

Periodically returning to the classroom as students permits teachers to refresh their memory of the learner's situation and the learning processes involved. Josephine Blagden (1988) notes several beliefs that were confirmed or revised when she submitted herself to a German course after teaching for a number of years. She was immediately aware of her vulnerability and the need to establish her identity in order to be relaxed and open to learning. Teacher attention to the students and their feelings more than the subject was crucial. Correction wrongly given was insulting and praise boosting. Her main criticism, however, was that *she* wasn't used enough. Here was a group of adults with interesting and varying backgrounds, with imaginations, dreams, and opinions that were ignored in favour of reading passages about insects. Blagden laments, 'What I found frustrating was that there was no attempt to make it relevant to us.'

Equally, if giving private lessons, one should take a few. The different observations already noted become even more noticeable as a student. Especially remarkable is the teacher to student talk ratio. When your private teacher monopolises the hour with personal chat you ask yourself, 'Do I talk like that during my lessons?' It's a good eye-opener for a teacher turned student to feel what it's like when her goals are not being fulfilled.

For my studies I often came across articles that I needed to read in German, Italian and Spanish. Although possessing an elementary oral ability in these languages that would get me through many situations (stumbling but successfully), my reading abilities were quite low. Thus, my main desire was to work through the articles that I wanted to understand and learn the vocabulary in them that would be repeated in similar articles. So I had a specific goal. However, I realised that I enjoyed speaking languages more than reading them. Thus, I decided to give the articles to different teachers, let them read them, and then give me a resumé orally so that we could discuss them. My pedagogical question was to what extent would my tutors be able to tune in to my needs and to what extent would I be able to control their teaching?

As my mountain bicycle was still my major means of transportation, I didn't want to pay someone as much as I charged and I was also interested in seeing to what degree students at the university would be sensitive to adjusting to my needs and those of 'unequal encounters'. Thus I found students to help me with my German, Italian and Spanish – and later with my beginning Japanese.

German – Paula

At first I gave Paula summaries of my work in English and asked her to give me a summary in German during the lesson. I recorded her first speaking about 'my' information. Then I tried giving the same summary in German, stopping the player between each phrase to confirm and adjust my pronunciation, etc. before recording. I listened to the tapes later and found my understanding improved but that I had over-estimated my ability to handle high level linguistics in formal German. Later I found articles on teaching techniques which were more down-to-earth, about which I could say more (be more fluent) and which I could enjoy discussing with Paula.

I wondered if my own 1/1 students were able to realise when material was too difficult and how to supply more suitable material. As a teacher I think that my seeing their frustration rise was an indication that the material was probably either too difficult or not interesting enough and that I should change. Rarely did students control all the materials to be exploited although they were encouraged to do so. (A notable exception being Mlle Flandres who always prepared her own piles of books, realia, and ideas.) I also wondered if they were able to make the teacher (me) change when they found materials unsuitable, or if the teacher persevered with unsuitable materials.

■ Observation 20

Students should be encouraged to select materials themselves although this is traditionally the teacher's role. They will usually be more motivated when they have the choice. However, the teacher needs to be sensitive enough to see when perhaps materials are too difficult and advise the student to change. (See Case 1: Ariane.)

I met Paula in a university classroom a few times, in my office a few times, and then in my home. She seemed naturally interested in the articles and would ask me to explain a few teaching concepts, provide some background, or give my opinion from time to time which boosted my ego considerably in a situation where I felt inferior. I also noticed my German became more fluent and I 'found' vocabulary that I didn't know I had. It confirmed to me that if the teacher could lead me into the right content material and stroke my ego by respecting my opinion then all my language abilities were suddenly brought out. In other words, I knew the content very well and I felt positive about myself because she valued the information that I could provide.

We got through a dozen articles in German for my research which was my primary goal. I sometimes wished, however, that it could have been more social and I found myself occasionally digressing or mischievously side-tracking my teacher. My ulterior motive was clearly social, not academic. I rather think, however, that everyone has this ulterior motive to some extent, even though it may not be consciously admitted. We all want to interact socially and feel good about ourselves.

■ Observation 21

Perhaps one of the ways to avoid frustration as a teacher is to recognise the students' need for social contact as well as their professed need to do serious work. Finally, if they can feel good socially they are more motivated to work longer and harder on the subject. In this way, more language learning will probably take place than if we try to make them 'learn the language alone and for itself', an amorphously fleeting shadow that only linguists seem to love chasing.

Italian – Donatella

Donatella and I met occasionally in a café for three months and I felt that I made enjoyable progress – that is to say, it was fun, social, and painless. Granted, I had fewer articles to read in Italian, the environment was more conducive to social conversation, and perhaps the Italian language and culture are just that way.

The first few lessons were strained and after each one I wrote down why I felt so. First of all, I don't think Donatella was sure exactly what kind of course I wanted and had never taught lessons, nor had had one in a café. This was my fault, perhaps, but also hers in not asking more directly what it was I was after. Thus, she was perhaps uncomfortable and I, not speaking Italian very well and insisting that that was the only language we could speak, was not capable of saying much. Sometimes the first few lessons she would also speak most of the time, without me understanding very much, perhaps because I became very efficient at giving comprehension and continuation signals. Although it might have seemed like an adult conversation to an observer my frustration level rose and self-esteem sunk as I felt stupid at not really understanding what apparently she thought I could understand.

Observation 22

Some students are good communicators in that they can feign understanding thus encouraging more input from the people they meet. However, they can sometimes do this too much and fan the flame of talk coming from a loquacious teacher. First perhaps, students need strategies as to how to get a speaker to adjust to their level efficiently ('I'm sorry, could you speak a bit slower' adding a strong accent). At the same time, a teacher should be more sensitive to the actual comprehension that is going on and distinguish between polite, ignorant attention and actual, interested comprehension.

Because there was no pressing urgency in my need of Italian, I felt less inclined to do any work at home, and it was easy to put off a meeting when other work piled up. After a few months, I simply stopped calling for appointments and when we happened to cross paths one day I explained that at the moment I had too many things on my agenda but that I would like to start up again when things quietened down. And I would, but I see I need a stronger motivation for me to learn Italian efficiently (a planned trip to Italy, having more Italian speakers around me, etc.).

Observation 23

Students dropping the 1/1 meetings after a while should not necessarily be taken as a sign that something was wrong with a teacher or her way of teaching. The good thing about most 1/1 is that it is ecologically self-regulating: if, for either of the parties, meetings become unwanted, for whatever reason, they can be discontinued – a very healthy option not available in public schools. Teachers hopefully see this as a good thing – for to teach people who don't want to be there is not only difficult, but often unpleasant.

Maria–Spanish

I met Maria at a social gathering and as we talked, I politely said I was very fond of Spanish, and displayed the few words I knew jokingly. She immediately gave me full attention and began speaking Spanish with me, simply, slowly and full of lovely intonation. Surprisingly enough I found myself understanding nearly everything she said and found I merely had to agree to keep her talking. When she did ask me questions they required only one word answers, usually *sí* or *no*.

I suddenly had the impression I was fluent, which I knew I wasn't. Later, I asked if she would let me invite her to lunch once a week in exchange for Spanish conversation. She agreed but said that she could pay for her own lunch.

Paying my tutors was a problem. All three at first refused to be paid for what they saw as mostly just enjoyable conversation. After I explained to Paula that it would have cost me a small fortune to have the German articles translated, she accepted a nominal SFrs. 20 an hour. I felt like I was nearly insulting Donatella when I tried to insist, so I just let it drop and bought her a nice gift after the last meeting. But I also felt as if there was less of a commitment on her part and a few meetings were postponed for little reason. The question of money probably was a contributing factor to the ending of the meetings.

I started meeting Maria after I had the experience with the other two and while I was doing the first draft of this book. I explained to her that I was serious about the meetings and I thought that I could learn a lot with her. However, my experience with other teachers was that if they didn't let me pay them, then they and I didn't take it seriously enough to be consistent. I told her, hoping to persuade her, that if she didn't let me pay her I would have to find someone else, but that I thought that she was a natural teacher and I would very much like to have conversation lessons with her. Finally, she reluctantly agreed to my paying for her lunch and a small fee. I'll never know, but I think it was this little bit of payment that made her, and me, more regular with the lessons.

■ Observation 24

An exchange of money for services rendered defines the meetings as valuable exchanges. Without it, lessons risk falling into rather artificial meetings between friends which may ultimately become uncomfortable for both parties because one doesn't know if they are professional or merely social. The difficulty that new teachers have in accepting money seems to be due to the social as opposed to skilful conception of how they use language every day. Mlle Flandres (Case 8) has always insisted on paying me even when I found it uncomfortable, saying 'I must pay, I want to be free.' I didn't really understand that at first. After being a student in the same situation, I think I do. She has to pay to keep the situation defined as she likes and to remain 'free' to control and lead the lessons where she wants them to go – something I had trouble doing with my teachers. (N.B. *Social* is used with two meanings. I believe in social interaction as a valid means to acquire language. However, in 1/1 teachers may be *professionally social* in that the teacher knows how to adjust well and gets paid for it. Without the pay the meetings become *merely social* and the student questions what it is the teacher is getting out of it, and the risk is that neither of them will take it seriously enough to make the communicating intense.)

Maria at first ventured to explain a few rules and to write a lot down for me. However, wanting principally conversation, I told her to relax and not worry about writing so much. Apparently she at first felt guilty for doing something that seemed so easy to her: communicating well. Later she relaxed and began to believe me when I said that I knew what kind of learner I was, and that simple conversation was the best thing.

Asako – Japanese (in the environment)

When I moved to Japan in April 1990 to teach at Nanzan University, I found myself in the situation of being a beginning language learner again. I again felt my distaste at the idea of returning to classes and was curious to see how much I could just pick up in the environment and learn on my own from books. The various people who volunteered help showed me again that some people are natural language teachers while others are naturally discouraging to the learner (or were at least to me) by the way they adjust, correct, and give confidence. Some will give you all the rules and the complete forms on a street corner when you're lost, while others will simply give you a word or two and great enthusiasm which makes you feel good about what you can do with the language already.

Soon I realised that I needed more contact with this latter sort of person if I was going to progress faster. So I began having various students exchange conversation time with me, ten minutes of English conversation and ten minutes of them helping me with Japanese. Through doing so I could spot the student that I felt could help me the most, Asako. Not that the others were bad, just that she seemed to reflect my way of learning and was willing to follow my learning strategies (let's go for a drink, now I'll teach you how to juggle in Japanese, OK?). That is, I could lead and she would follow with enthusiasm and language adjusted to my beginning level. I arranged more regular meetings of forty-five minutes three or four times a week and again had to insist on paying her. I asked for language that I could immediately use with the office staff, my tennis partners and my landlord. Asako provided me with immediately useful language that was reinforced when I used it away from her.

The first few weeks with Asako were mostly in English (How can I say . . .) with a lot of translating, but gradually it came to be about 50 per cent in Japanese with set routines (Come in. Please sit down. Would you like something to drink? etc.). For the summer break I asked her to record all my Japanese notes on a cassette with long pauses and music in the background. That way I was able to review periodically what I had already half-way learned while in Europe for two months. The music and gentle voice were so pleasing that I played it many times without really listening, simply for background music. I was pleasantly surprised when returning in September that I hadn't forgotten much.

Because of my busy schedule, I love the flexibility of someone coming to my office for forty-five minutes several times a week and of my being able to say what I want to learn and how I want to do it.

3 Views from other teachers

Interaction leads to an exciting broadening of perspectives. Don't take my word for it, try it. Go and talk to people and imagine you are in their shoes. That's what this chapter is about. We are many times more rich when we give what we have to give, because things always seem to come back multiplied.

In the last several years I have interviewed over twenty-five other 1/1 teachers who have confirmed much of what I was doing but also provided me with many new ideas and perspectives. The variety of their experiences provides a broader base on which to evaluate one's own teaching and provides alternative ways of doing and looking at things. The few examples outlined here are not meant as a complete, nor realistic, representation of the variety in the field, but nevertheless provide some divergent examples.

1 Independent teachers

Carla, in Basel, Switzerland, married a Swiss and began teaching private lessons while hunting for a full time job as a sports teacher in a regular school. Although she had no EFL training whatsoever, she is an extremely pleasant and enthusiastic person and has the natural capacity to tune into people. Carla was teaching about twelve students 1/1 when she finally found her position as a sports instructor and had to drop all but a few.

At first Carla only charged SFrs. 20 an hour, explaining, 'I'd feel guilty asking more. All we usually do is sit around talking and drinking coffee.' Her personal investment with her students was such that one student even loaned a summer house in the mountains to Carla and her husband for a week's holiday.

Another student, rather eccentric, often wasn't in the mood for speaking English and Carla would simply end up playing cards with her or helping her wrap up Christmas presents. Carla now charges SFrs. 30 an hour but admits that they are such social meetings that it often runs into several hours and she still charges only SFrs. 30. She plans to do a summer EFL course once 'to get some background' because she enjoys it so much.

■■■ Observation 25
In 1/1 language teaching, the personality of the teacher is very important. Learning EFL methodology, although generally providing useful tools, may lead to artificial 'teacherese' rather than the naturally efficient interaction many untrained teachers are

already capable of. The ideal teacher is of course a highly trained teacher who also remains empathetic and broadminded. However, the trained teacher runs the danger of turning her potentially rich encounters into abstract 'classes'. Interaction with communicators who adjust well seems to be the most fertile ground for acquisition. Training can help, but may also get in the way at times.

A question for teachers in many areas to ponder might be, 'Have we outsmarted ourselves by being overtrained in the abstraction of our subject and in trying to teach that abstraction (when simply doing things with it is its natural pedagogy)?' At least, as the old adage goes, 'No method has yet been invented that will keep a child from learning something.' (Although we may not know what that 'something' is.) **Christianne** is a student at the university to whom I sent two Americans for private French tutoring. Both the wife and husband were doing research, she in music, he in linguistics. Christianne was a good choice as she was studying linguistics and was also at the music conservatory.

As she had never conducted private lessons, I explained briefly how I conducted my meetings and that her students would probably want to talk about what they were good at and enjoyed. Her students were, to a certain extent, to teach Christianne about their research in these two areas and she was to help them do it, in French – an equal exchange. (She also later confessed to slight feelings of guilt about accepting money while she learned so much and had a good time.)

They first met at the university cafeteria for the noncommittal 'possibility' of lessons. The couple decided to meet separately since Mrs Music's level was somewhat higher.

Christianne met Mr Linguist in cafés where he seemed relaxed and felt free to converse. He often asked Christianne how he would persuade a colleague of certain things in French and Christianne would write the argument down and he would try it out on her, from which a discussion would ensue. He was doing with her what he wanted to do with other researchers at the university but without the risk, and with a great amount of help. He would often go to do his errands in town with her and they would talk as they walked, stopping at a café occasionally.

Christianne's lesson with Mrs Music was transferred from the café to a small study room in the university so she could practise reading out loud. However, whenever anyone came into the room Mrs Music would stop speaking. After a few weeks, the meetings were taken to her home. Christianne took her violin and they played together. Christianne was awed by Mrs Music's musical ability on the piano and showed due respect in a somewhat simplified, but far from condescending, French. Mrs Music's confidence and positive self-image carried over from her music and French became less of a struggle because of the intense communication taking place concerning music.

■ Observation 26

Doing things with the target language may intensify the learning experience and make it easier because of the natural concrete referents (see page 57) offered by the situations (as opposed to the abstractions too often offered in 'sit and imagine' classes).

Alessia, an Italian who has taught a variety of students both English and Italian in North and South America and in Italy, came up with an interesting list of observations when I spoke with her:

1 A good teacher is above all a good natural psychologist.
2 For a beginning teacher, it is better to have students who have no pressure from exams. While exam teaching may appear to be easiest because you have a set amount of material and a motivated student, the material may be uninteresting and the student purely motivated to pass a test, not to learn to communicate. Stress may be very high.
3 You can't just teach language. Contributing toward a student's maturity and information stock are just as important as language learning.
4 Teaching must be tailor-made for the needs of the students and adapted to their age, sex, and background.
5 Non-native speaking teachers should use recordings of native speakers.

I think observations 1–4 can be seen in the other case studies. However the last, 5, needs some discussion, especially for non-native readers.

Pronunciation insecurity seems a fairly common trait among non-native teachers. They often admit to being afraid that if students listen only to them they may pick up their foreign accent in English. I feel this is an exaggerated concern. In fact, learning English from a non-native may be preferable for several reasons. The most obvious reason is that they usually know the native language of the speaker and can predict the difficulties that are relevant using contrastive analysis and their own experience.

Also, it may not be advisable to accustom oneself solely to a native speaker accent if one is going to be doing international business. A German who is importing Japanese products will usually be interacting in English. According to the latest statistics, people who speak English as a second language in the world outnumber the native speakers by four to one. Other things being equal, one has an 80 per cent chance of meeting and speaking English to a non-native as opposed to only a 20 per cent chance of speaking to a native. Perhaps it will be necessary in the future for even native speakers of English to learn a neutral form of international English to handle international affairs. Many non-native teachers may have more of a neutral accent than many natives. This is not an argument against native speakers as teachers, only an argument against the myth that native speakers are always the best source for a reliable norm. In fact a native speaker may have a restricted regional accent which may be little understood elsewhere. Both natives and non-natives can be excellent teachers; to place too much emphasis on this criterion, and by implication pronunciation, is to underestimate the more important qualities that make a teacher effective.

Aside

I once did a simple experiment with a class of my university students. I played them excerpts of five presentations from international conferences and I asked them to try to say where the speakers were from and to rate them on intelligibility: 1 = incomprehensible, 5 = totally comprehensible. Two were Americans, two were British, and one was Dutch. They guessed the origins of the American and British speakers but were split between America, England, and Canada for the Dutchman. But what was really amazing was that the Dutchman scored as high as or higher than the native speakers on intelligibility. Apparently, he had a neutral accent, difficult to place, and more understandable than most natives. For me that is a desirable profile of the ability of an international speaker – nativeness is not the goal, being internationally neutral with extensive intelligibility is preferable.

Alessia's observation number 5 is not wrong; for me, however, it should just be rephrased to say that *all* teachers should use recordings of a variety of native and non-native speakers. One of the dangers in 1/1 is that the student may become too used to the teacher's speech, and the teacher too used to understanding that of the students. They understand each other easily even when other natives might not. Especially with the occasional student who feels she knows it all, tapes may inspire some humility. Having family and friends interact with students is also an eye-opening experience for both teacher and learner. It is then that we see how efficient we have become at understanding our students' English, and how with other speakers communication can break down more easily.

Susan has taught 1/1 for over ten years in a small city in Switzerland. Although kept busy with two teenage children and a husband who is also a teacher, she actively develops herself in other areas, such as women's studies and transactional analysis (see below), which she admits stimulates her own teaching a lot. She has had most of her students for a number of years, some as long as six or seven. Students usually sign up for monthly or yearly periods, and then make extensions as they wish.

At the time that I interviewed her she had six single students (a doctor, a high school student, two business people, and two housewives) and two small groups (two businessmen together twice a week and one group of three women). She had never done any advertising and had got her students by word of mouth. When others had asked for lessons she refused for lack of time. She often referred them to other private teachers that she knew, but admitted there were some teachers doing it that she didn't recommend. She saw the market as greatly untapped.

She sets up her classes to correspond to the public school dates so she can be with her family during holidays. Students come at regular weekly times to her home where lessons are conducted in the family's office or living room. The businessmen schedule from one meeting to the next as they are often travelling. However, she feels the regular times give her students some security and that being flexible is only natural for the travelling business people. She uses books (*Kernel* and others) often, except with the businessmen who bring their own documents to work on. Lesson planning she does from one lesson to the next.

Susan sees her major problem as raising prices with students that she has had so long that they have become very good friends. She also recognises that for some students the social contact, as with a club, is more important than the language learning, and that having the lessons degenerate into interesting 'talk' is actually the unspoken goal for some. Finally, she considers her students as friends and gets quite attached to them, as I could tell by her animated description of them.

Susan uses transactional analysis (TA) which has proved useful for other people as well. (See Wright, 1987, for a brief introduction to its usefulness as a way of seeing how problems might occur in interaction, or Berne, 1964, for the original.) Basically, TA describes three different personalities in each person that may be communicating at any one time, parent, adult and child. In a conversation, one assumes one of these roles and assumes that the other person will be in one of these roles. When the two people's assumptions are very different, then problems in communication might occur.

For example, a student might think of herself as a child while learning and expect to be communicated to from a parent authority figure. ('I don't know anything, correct everything I do wrong.') But the teacher may want an adult–adult situation. ('I won't say you are wrong, as I wouldn't with anyone I respect, but I will help you to reformulate.') In such a case, the student may question the teacher's ability to teach, since it does not correspond to her conception of the roles. What usually happens then is that either the teacher will finally respond to the student's child as a parent, or the student will come round and be an adult. A third possibility would be that they continue to miscommunicate.

Barry is a young man who makes his living from teaching principally 1/1. He has high visibility as he advertises widely in his city newspaper and hangs posters offering personalised courses. His publicity is always accompanied by the same rather humorous cartoon of a British gentleman. His telephone recorded message when a client calls is all in English. It scares away beginners, in whom he's not interested, and those not highly motivated, who would be frightened anyway by his high fee. The authentically serious and intermediate are impressed by the message and either leave a message or can call him when he's in to arrange a meeting. Although he started it as a way to support his studies two years ago, it has been so successful that he has temporarily put his university studies on hold.

2 Teachers in language schools

I had the opportunity to interview several expatriate English teachers in Italy who were working in various large cities in private language schools. All said they gave 1/1 lessons but did so in slightly different circumstances.

Rachel was the only one who said her boss allowed the teachers in the school to organise their own private lessons with students, to charge and collect fees. They were also allowed to use the rooms and materials in the school.

Other teachers had employers who insisted that all private lessons came through them, since the school was their legal employer. However, a few teachers admitted to meeting students away from school to give lessons that the employer did not know about, charging less than what the school charged (making it cheaper for the student) and earning more than what the school offered them for 1/1 lessons. Apparently the school often kept from 40 to 60 per cent of the fee, with the remainder going to the teacher.

Rick said he taught thirty hours a week, eighteen class hours and twelve private 1/1 meetings that the school didn't know about. He admitted that 60 per cent of his income came from his private lessons. Most of these he said were conversation lessons in which the student decided what was to be done. 'With some I could ask one question at the beginning and need think no more about what materials to use. But I had a few who were pushed into lessons by their parents or boss; it was murder trying to get them to interact sometimes.'

The next two sections look at organisations that seem a lot fairer towards teachers. The first is a 1/1 service and the second is a school owned by the teachers.

3 A 1/1 service company

Two public school teachers in Geneva started a 1/1 service business, CIWA, in 1986. The idea was originally to tutor high school students in any subject at the student's home. Geneva is a diplomatic city with a lot of foreign families moving to and from it every year. The public school system has to accommodate students from many different countries with many different backgrounds and doesn't have all the resources needed, or desired by the parents, to ensure success at school. Thus the service CIWA offers has a ready market and has since grown to be recommended to concerned parents by school authorities.

However, because CIWA was open to go wherever the demand showed itself, their client-profile has changed somewhat since they started: now one third of their work is composed of language tutoring in the business sector, one sixth is leisure courses (piano, painting, etc.), and three sixths is still tutoring high school students trying to catch up or re-adapt to different school systems in a variety of subjects, mostly languages.

Daniel Wack, director and coordinator, says he hires experienced teachers, or students at the university who have had experience, apparently with the basic requirement being that they be charming and get good reports back from parents. Daniel admits he is extremely careful about hiring reliable, professional, and personable teachers. They do no training although there is guidance when problems occur and a stock of skeleton outlines for different courses from public schools is available.

The first year the business totalled about 160 hours a month, the second year 300 hours. Daniel presently has thirty teachers teaching between ten and sixty hours a month. The normal length of a private tutoring course is from three to nine months. He stresses to his clients that he is offering short term courses to help students to catch up or to prepare for specific goals. They are not intended to replace school for high school students, but to help them temporarily when they need special attention. He has built up good rapport with school administrators by meeting with them and clarifying that he wishes to work in conjunction with the teachers to help the individual students to progress. Needless to say, this is also an excellent form of publicity.

All organising is done by phone and Daniel works out of his home, thus there is no office or school rent to pay. Fees are between SFrs. 45 and SFrs. 50 (depending on the age of the student and the subject being taught; see appendix 6 for exchange rates) per forty-five minutes, with reductions for signing up for a large number of hours (1988 figures). The company takes care of the governmental paperwork for pension and insurance, finds the work for the teachers and the teacher gets SFrs. 32 an hour. About 80 per cent of the courses are given at the student's home, 15 per cent in business surroundings, and 5 per cent in public libraries.

Daniel sees three big selling points that he has: **1** he offers tailor-made teachers, specialised with experience, willing to adapt to the student **2** the teacher goes to the student's own home or business, and **3** the hours can be arranged flexibly between the student and the teacher. He matches up teachers with students on the basis of student needs and teacher abilities and preferences, and their proximity to each other in the city.

I asked Daniel what he saw as the necessary requirements for setting up such a business and what he thought the future was. He said that it would probably work in any international city where there were families coming and going regularly and where there was a university to provide part-time qualified teachers. As for the future he foresees a natural continual development for his high school clientele. However the business sector is potentially the greatest and seems relatively untapped. He feels that his total hours will expand to 500 a month in the next few years.

4 Teacher-owned 1/1 schools

The Bergmann Language School in Biel, Switzerland is owned and operated by the teachers teaching there. The school itself, a corporation, earns money on the classes that are taught there, but they also allow their teachers to use the premises for 1/1 teaching with just a small percentage going to the school. About 40 per cent of the total teaching for the eleven part time and three full time teachers is 1/1. They offer an 'à la carte' service in which students in 1/1 can plan and programme the content and methodology of their own courses, saying what they want to learn and how.

Courses are naturally most in demand in the evening. To encourage daytime hours, there are cheaper rates. Teachers find that they generally start out giving lessons on the premises of the school but that they sometimes subsequently move to a café or restaurant as students become more conversationally comfortable with learning a language through interaction, and leaving more space at the school for other teachers and students. The teachers are free to teach as they see best, and are at the same time offered in-house teacher training sessions.

The idea of teachers owning and directing their own school is intuitively very appealing to me. Many teachers dream of the independence and responsibility that comes with operating your own business and all of its facets. When it's yours, you invest more of yourself in its success, you don't just put in your hours and go home. Doing it alone may be a lonely and dangerous task, however. Doing it with other teachers is easier not only because of the shared labour but because of the variety of input, the flexibility that many people as opposed to one can have, and the interaction that makes you grow professionally. You are more concerned about yourself and the school growing in quality. A professional investment is thus doubly profitable: first for the teacher, and secondly for the school which is partially owned by the teacher.

I have discovered two small, British-based, teacher-owned, language schools which concentrate on 1/1 (there may be many more that I am not aware of). The first, English Immersion Courses, has been run by Keith and Ruth Carr in their own home since 1981 (Portswood, Southampton). Their advertising brochure promises 'total flexibility', 'a course designed for you alone', 1/1 teaching which makes 'the best use of your time', and living with the teachers. The slick brochure, their prices (£950 for fifteen hours in five days, or to be arranged) and their offer of telex and telefax services, so that clients can stay in touch with their companies if they wish, indicate they are aiming at upper management business people.

While the Carrs offer 1/1 for many of the reasons that the previous chapters have argued for, a second school, The English Experience (Lyminge, Kent), offers a more folksy brochure and seems to use more action English techniques (see Chapter 5) and social contact. Taught by Mark Fletcher, with the administrative and social programme organised by Richard Mums, they describe what they do as 'more than a language course' as they try to integrate students into their own lives: 'You come with us (as friends – not as tourists) to our favourite places.' They offer twelve-day courses at £560 (with reductions for married couples and groups), maximum six students on any course, suggestopedia and accelerated learning techniques, sports, pubs, and parties.

Both the above schools seem concerned with teaching the whole person in a social environment through a multitude of activities. They are not constrained by the concept that learning only takes place in classrooms and they appear to be extremely flexible as to the student's desires, needs, and level.

Finally, another option is a home stay with a tutor, similar to the two described above, but organised through a national or international concern. I have seen several such advertising blurbs in the past few years, one reportedly in business since 1979. They offer flexibility in the number of hours for course work and the place one wants to go. Of course, it remains to be seen what exactly they mean by qualified teachers. However, the apparent success of such organisations does show that the 1/1 configuration and 'living a language' is attractive to many students and that it is a viable business endeavour.

5 The views of teacher-trainers

Wilberg, to my knowledge was the first person to speak of 1/1, at the 1986 IATEFL conference. He subsequently published a book *One to One* in the summer of 1987. He stresses using the student and the student's needs, and the giving of space to the student to learn, which I find very positive. Apparently he sees little relevance, however, in the mass of interaction research that has been done. He provides no bibliography nor further sources for teachers and seems to describe principally multiple-hour intensive 1/1 teaching in a school setting. While such a structure does have its advantages, and the book some good advice, I would guess that there are relatively few teachers who actually do 1/1 in a school and fewer who offer multiple-hour intensive 1/1.

Smit, at the 1987 IATEFL conference in Belgium, gave an interesting presentation entitled 'Individual vs. group teaching to business executives'. She stated that the practice of 1/1 teaching is extremely widespread, although it has been greatly unrecognised and ignored by research and publications (she offered no statistics).

		1/1 (individual lessons)	groups of two or more
1	**Location**	can be anywhere	must have a classroom
2	**Ages**	generally older	younger age groups
3	**Tempo of class**	the teacher can adjust to the student's level	teacher aims at the middle level
4	**Hierarchy**	two professionals on equal terms	teacher has power over the students
5	**Structure**	immense flexibility to adjust the course to the student	group teaching is inflexible
6	**Scheduling**	totally flexible	totally inflexible
7	**Price**	costs more, but often charged to company and/ or tax deductible	cheaper by the head

(Smit 1987)

Defining groups as two or more students with a teacher, she proceeds to outline seven principle differences between individuals and groups as shown in the table on the previous page.

Although I would agree with the differences generally, I feel that perhaps the group characteristics are a bit too harshly drawn. There can be flexibility in time, place, structure, and tempo and the teacher of groups can learn more of this from teaching individuals (see Chapter 7). That is, we might try treating our groups more as many separate individuals, which they are.

Smit says that students are prepared to pay three times as much for private lessons because of the possibility to adjust the tempo, structure and scheduling. They also appreciate that they have a 'sanctuary which is encouraging, a teacher who is tactful, and a consultation which is private'. Something like a doctor or lawyer, the 1/1 teacher is a consultant in whom the client has trust and this trust should be respected. She gives two to four hour blocks of lessons at a time and often deals with students coming for intensive short courses.

Smit gives successful 1/1 teachers the following characteristics and prefers not to call them 'managers':

a they have total command of their subject
b they have inexhaustible materials
c they have knowledge of business terminology
d they are as much a professional as is the client and must use diplomacy and be discreet

I thoroughly agree with **d** but again would say that **a–c** need qualification.

First **a**, no one has 'total' command of a subject. In fact, that is what continual teacher development is all about, improving our knowledge about the subject and our ability to help others acquire it.

Secondly **b**, Smit laments the lack of materials and states that most coursebooks are made for the 18–24 age group and that the conversations are too colloquial. Materials, in my opinion, spring from the student and his or her environment. ESP courses have been extremely effective in using such materials. Too many pre-made materials for 1/1 teaching would defeat its most important and viable feature, its adaptability. The student is the first 'inexhaustible' resource. (See Chapter 5 for further discussion of materials.)

Thirdly **c**, knowledge of business terminology will certainly be useful, but it would be unreasonable to expect that any one teacher would know all the specialised vocabulary for the many different domains of international business. One should have humility and allow the student to teach the teacher at times. As already noted, learning about the student's 'subject' is what makes for natural communicative exchanges and the establishment of equal encounters. Knowing vocabulary also does not presuppose that we know the processes and mechanisms involved. Many people have a reading understanding of the terms 'stocks' and 'bonds' without ever understanding the processes leading to their buying, selling and dumping.

Four well-attended 1/1 workshops were given by Neithammer and Murray during 1987/88 to different branches of the English Teachers Association Switzerland. Some of the advantages of 1/1 that they mention are:

1 No 'group control' problems.
2 No competition for the teacher's attention, i.e. no student conflicts of interest as the student gets an individualised course.
3 Student can take the initiative.
4 Tape recorder can be used to record student. Feedback is always interesting.
5 No visibility problems (blackboard, pictures).

These advantages are not necessarily absent from classroom teaching but may simply be more difficult to achieve.

Some of the problems with 1/1 that they mention are:

1 It may be too intensive for the student (pressure, tension).
2 The student may not get enough exposure to the same thing or enough opportunity to practise the same thing over and over.
3 It may be boring: 'just the two of us'.
4 Course books have many activities for groups and pairs.

I feel problem 1 is something teachers should consider seriously. Students are often not used to being 'on-line' for a complete hour. They can relax somewhat while others take the stage in a class, and so can the teacher. If the teacher teaches in an intensive classroom manner, the student will quickly tire, especially in intensive courses. A more relaxed, but still alert, atmosphere needs to be created in which there is a reduction of stress. We can allow them time out by doing activities that demand only slight monitoring on their part and little production. The teacher can tell a comprehensible story without any questions at the end, they can both listen to some music or a song for a few minutes and not base their subsequent discussion on interpreting the words but on how the music made them feel. A variation between pleasant, known review material and new, challenging material can also signal a shift in intensity; flowing into the first kind when the student is looking tired and frustrated can give them the courage and confidence to try the new material again.

I see problems 2 and 3 as possible even with large classes, although I understand Murray and Neithammer's fear as well. Exposure to items in many different forms is difficult anywhere. Of course with fewer people, there are not as many choices of personalities that you can be attracted to. But that doesn't mean that you can't exploit other people who aren't there (as they pointed out in their workshop), in literature, poems, stories and newspapers; or people that are close to the students: friends, family, etc.; or as with my two young students talking about women, or using video clips with adolescents. And finally problem 4, coursebooks which describe pair activities in my opinion are ideal for teaching 1/1. The teacher simply takes the place of one of the students. That allows the teacher to see first hand whether it is interesting or not and whether it produces the desired language.

In 1987 International House, Hastings, were the first, to my knowledge, to offer an extensive 'Five-day TEFL Workshop' on 1/1 teaching, which for me is a sign that teacher-trainers and administrators are recognising its viability and popularity as an alternative to group/class teaching. Their information sheet for the workshop explains 'One-to-one teaching plays an important role in certain areas of TEFL, yet the art of this form of teaching remains relatively unexplored.' Their proposed programme highlights several of the areas which we have already covered and leads in nicely to the following chapters.

Programme (One-to-one workshop, International House, Hastings, April 27, 1987)

The main programme comprises 28 lesson-periods of seminars and workshop sessions, covering:
- Activities and approaches appropriate to one-to-one teaching;
- The development of a clear understanding of the unique dynamics of one-to-one teaching and how the various elements can be exploited to the maximum advantage of both learner and teacher;
- Analysing language and learning needs and setting the highest realisable objectives;
- Planning a course that fulfils such objectives;
- Examining the relationships between teacher and learner, and subsequent flexibility in the learner and teacher roles;
- Using the environment, be it in-company, or in-school, or at home, to create a positive and stimulating learning environment;
- Choice and exploitation of materials.

4 A framework for tuning in

This chapter presents some tentative conclusions, concerning what was seen in Chapters 2 and 3, and a practical framework for approaching 1/1 teaching.

1 Tentative conclusions

The first thing to notice in the case studies is that the first two students, Ariane and Maria, had distinctly different motives from the others for learning and practising English: passing a test. That is, they were being evaluated on their ability and they were going to be told if they succeeded or failed. The others were not.

Ariane's and Maria's motivation for having the lessons was not instrumental or integrative, merely incidental. For them 'getting ahead in life was a central goal and the learning of [a language] was incidental, just another school subject. . . .' (Gardner and Lambert 1972:140).

Although the books Ariane and Maria were studying could have been instrumentally motivating (and they were somewhat for Maria), they were forced into being merely incidentally relevant due to the students' overpowering motivation to pass their exams. This is a case where too much pressure from evaluation inhibits learning. Not that it is wrong to want to pass one's exams. But here, perhaps, a class of students with a teacher may be just as efficient since the text and information are the motivation of the entire group, divorced from individual needs and instrumental motivation. In most everyday conversation, the people are the most important and then comes the information. In school, it seems often that the information is more important than the students. In language learning this need not be so.

The aspect of evaluation and the effect it has is very important. In the later 1/1 encounters, none of the students was going to be linguistically evaluated at a later date. They would of course be evaluated on their work, which one hoped would be improved by their acquired language abilities. The point here is that the language is not evaluated but rather what they do with it. This is closely paralleled in some language pedagogies, such as Total Physical Response (see Asher, 1977), in which students are actually doing things.

2 A few more ski analogies

I learned to teach skiing by learning how to ski. Supposedly hired as a bus driver my first Christmas in Switzerland, I was asked to fill in as a ski teacher. They were kind enough to give me the beginning group since, coming from Florida, I had only skied six days in my life. I was basically one step ahead of my students and learned as they did. We just enjoyed ourselves, falling and playing games as we learned. The camp director was so impressed with the happy kids, who all said they wanted to come again, that I was hired back for Easter and Christmas for the next four years.

We found out that kids could learn skiing just as well with leaders who amused them, safely, as with professional ski instructors who might not be as playful. And the kids enjoyed it more. The director asked himself a few simple questions: Which teacher is better for the kids? Which teacher is cheaper?

A few years ago I had a thirteen-year-old nephew visit me in the spring and I took him skiing. I thought, '*Voilà*! Here's a great 1/1 opportunity to teach skiing.' Little did I know how poorly I would do, and how important it was to realise why afterwards.

The first run down, he had a great time. The second run I began with some gentle instructions 'bend your knees', 'weight forward'. At every turn I looked back to see what new piece of information or corrective advice I could give him. Two runs like that, with his frustration growing at each tumble, and he was in tears! What happened to the great ski teacher (me) who learned so quickly how to ski and was valued and well-paid in a world-famous ski resort? Couldn't I even teach my own nephew how to ski? 'The fault must be his,' I thought, 'tender boy!' He stopped for a while and later went skiing for the rest of the day with a (non-teacher) friend of mine and had great fun!

What had happened was that I had turned evaluator, not fun-loving uncle. I had wanted to help him so much that I was correcting every little thing he did and giving him so much information that his brain was on overload. (Many of you may recognise the displaced ambition that a parent often torments a child with.) He wasn't enjoying skiing with me, he was thinking about all the details that I was telling him and how I was constantly watching him and going to correct him. Being constantly evaluated is not fun.

I thought back, do I teach like that with my ski classes? I realised I didn't, that I usually gave a bit of instruction early on and then skied a lot and played games that would have them learning without being evaluated. I did give direct lessons to each as they traded places to be the first to follow me down. But that was one run out of twenty in a day. Periodically during the day I would bring up points that might help them if they were ready to incorporate them (the student learns when she is ready), but then I was using group discourse and not direct evaluation and judging. They didn't feel my 'heavy eye' forever on them. Instead, they were concentrating on doing something with their skis, having fun, something that was natural and probably teaching them more than my instructions anyway.

The above story may look like a criticism of 1/1 teaching with the conclusion being that teaching groups with group discourse may be better. It is true that if we transfer our normal group teaching strategies to the 1/1 situation, this is a valid criticism. What I'm trying to say is that we don't use the same strategies in the two situations if we want the students to benefit maximally. The danger for regular classroom teachers in 1/1 situations is that they may overload a student with correction and information. In small quantities it may be fine, but doing something with the language is much more efficient, natural and fun in language acquisition. The advantages that are available in 1/1 are negligible if we act like classroom teachers and use group discourse strategies. Our experience as classroom teachers can be very valuable in 1/1 situations but it can also get in the way. On the other hand, our knowledge of 1/1 encounters and their benefits can be put to use in the classroom (see Chapter 7).

Many people do like to be evaluated periodically, to know where they are, but not continually, and not through corrections that interfere with their meaningful communicating. People want to use language instrumentally and functionally, not merely as abstract information to be evaluated. It is the experience of overevaluation and demeaning correction that produces many 'classophobics' who refuse to go back to what many see as 'impractical school daze'.

Summary of principal ideas

present a low-evaluative, supporting environment to reduce anxiety
tune in, adjust to, and use your students' interests and motivations
equalise the encounter by making the students into teachers of things they know well
present enough schoolishness to satisfy their learned conventional needs about lessons

---

3 A framework for tuning in with new clients

There are five practical questions with several sub-categories that a 1/1 teacher needs to think about when beginning with any new client.

1 Who is the client?
2 Where will we be meeting?
3 When and how long will we be meeting?
4 What are the goals and needs (what is to be learned)?
5 How will we do it (what methods and techniques)?

4 Who

Of central concern is whom one is teaching. Answering this question with the proper depth will, of course, lead into the others. Of course we want to know as much as possible about the student before teaching in order to prepare adequately, but much of our authentic teaching will also include getting to know clients better during the course in order to adjust to them ever more efficiently. We will want to know, but at the same time will be continually attuned to shifts in, the client's motivation, experience, expectations, needs, and personality.

5 Where

Where lessons are given dictates to a degree what can be done. Each place will have advantages and restrictions that the others won't have. As we saw in the case histories, the place may help the creation of an equal encounter, depending on whose territory is used.

Six **where**s (but there may be more):

  i in a school
 ii the teacher's home
iii the client's home
 iv the client's place of work
  v in a café or restaurant
 vi on the move in an activity (e.g. taking a walk, visiting a museum, or skiing)

Language schools often implicitly give the impression of professional credibility immediately, but 'classophobics' might shy away from them. It's nice to have access to all the materials, technology and quiet rooms you need, but for intensive multiple hour lessons, it's nice to get away from the school occasionally. In a school, the method may be dictated by the administration. However, many teachers report that they have more or less a free hand, although they are encouraged to use the school method and text. It seems some directors of schools don't see 1/1 as very important to their business, while others cultivate it. A further advantage of schools is that they usually handle all administration (advertising, scheduling, billing, retirement pay, etc.) and the teacher is free to concentrate on teaching. However they usually demand a sizable percentage of the fee for doing all this.

The teacher's home seems to be most often used by women who have married or moved abroad with their husbands and got into giving lessons at first only occasionally. As they get more students, they become very professional. One very apparent advantage to teaching at home is having one's stock of books and files handy so that adaptation of materials is not limited to what you can carry in your briefcase. Homes provide comfort and convenience but the immediate impression of professionalism that comes with a 'school' may not be present. Thus it is often built into everything else, from course organisation to detailed accounting. Teachers try to schedule classes when the kids are at school, they may take the phone off the hook, they might even try to make the living room or kitchen look very much like a school class (even refusing to serve coffee as this might lead students to believe they are not serious). I feel this professionalism is a good thing but may be overdone and may work against the advantages that a home has to offer. Of course, such independent teachers handle all methodological and administrative choices unless attached to a 1/1 service (see Chapter 3, section 3 and 4).

The student's home may be transformed somewhat in the same way as the teacher's when they have invited their teacher over. Here the same problems of professionalism and interference from family and phone may arise. Students do seem to appreciate the teacher being flexible enough to come to them, although the question of who pays for transportation when the teacher goes to the student can be problematic. As we saw, this flexibility on the part of the teacher can be a major selling point.

The student's place of work may be a much more logical place to hold a lesson, especially if one is learning for the job. Some businesses set aside special rooms for training or you may be asked to give your lessons in an office. Here again one risks interruption by telephone messages or the student's clients. There are some published materials on in-company teaching which are a subset of ESP (English for Specific, or Special, Purposes) a domain that merits the attention of 1/1 teachers in these situations. That the teacher can come to the student is attractive to many busy business people and potentially the greatest market for 1/1.

A café or restaurant lesson offers the advantages of putting the participants into a natural social situation but demands other measures (discussed in the case histories) to ensure professionalism and to avoid the impression of just talking. This environment also allows the student and teacher to meet in neutral territory and to equalise the encounter with behaviour dictated by the social surroundings (i.e. there is less teacherese possible). Students may be fearful, however, of meeting someone they know. Or they might be embarrassed about their English and being overheard in public. Avoiding the places they usually frequent takes care of the first, finding quiet, relatively empty cafés pretty much handles the second. However, if the communicating is intense they usually forget where they are anyway. And many, I find, like to be overheard speaking English as it is rather prestigious for them. Nevertheless, there will be times when it gets a bit loud, or friends do find you or your client. Instead of seeing these always as distractions, they can often be used positively if we think creatively (e.g. we talk about the noise, or the person who interrupted you, how do you excuse yourself politely from such situations, what would you say in English?).

Performing some activity with a student, such as playing tennis, visiting a museum, or simply taking a walk may prove to be the most rewarding for some because of the natural concrete referents available. Doing something with language that is not abstract is very positive for lower levels. Of course some may feel that this is not a language lesson despite evidence that a large portion of early acquisition takes place faster while they are actively doing something. This may be because they often forget they are communicating in English.

We normally teach in one of these places or another. However, changing occasionally to add variety, and to experiment with how it affects you and your students, may be advisable. Changing locales is especially advisable with short-term intensive teaching as we may tire of one environment and the language may become associated with only one setting. But finally, 'the social meaning of a context is constructed through the social interaction that takes place between the participants' (Light and Perret-Clermont, 1986).

In other words, learning can take place anywhere with the proper rapport and interaction. The people, what they do, and how they do it are the major factors.

A second 'where' question refers to the positioning in a room or at a table. Most teachers seem to prefer to sit facing a student across a table that's not too big. However, when teaching in a conference room in a bank where the tables are usually huge, manoeuvering your client onto a corner of the table will make it easier for both of you to look at documents. Sitting side by side can give you a stiff neck and it makes eye contact difficult. When possible, however, let your client choose where to sit in a café and where she wants you to sit.

6 When

The **when** of language teaching includes at what time of day, for how many minutes or hours, and the duration of the course if it isn't simply from one meeting to the next. Many beginning teachers take on clients first on a once a week basis either with set meeting times or with flexible ones, arranged from one meeting to the next. Some may jump straight into intensive short term lessons in which a student wants many hours in a short period in preparation for a precise goal. Of course it is a continuum between long-distance, once in a while, meetings and intensive short term courses. The flexible teacher will be willing to adapt to the needs and desires of the client.

A further consideration is the length of the meetings, thirty minutes, an hour, several hours, or a full day for several days in intensive courses. For longer courses, especially, we need to be concerned with variety and the fatigue of the student. Needless to say, the amount and frequency of lessons will to a certain extent determine the goals set and the methods to use.

The when and how often affect rates with some teachers. Scheduling multiple hours may come with a reduction and teaching in the evening, peak time, may cost more.

7 What

What exactly you will be teaching depends on the answers to the preceding questions of who, where, and when, but can also be dealt with directly by asking the student or employer what the goals and needs are. These of course may change as the student changes or as the teacher realises what is needed and feasible. ESP has extensive literature on doing needs analysis. A simple questionnaire at the first meeting can serve both the purpose of a teaching tool and of gathering information about the student's background, language goals and desires. The personal characteristics can be exploited later.

Allwright (1982) makes a difference between needs, wants and lacks and provides two questionnaires: one in which the students express their needs and another to discern the students' preference for ways to go about it (see Dickinson, 1987 for copies of these forms). The idea here is that what a student thinks she needs and wants may be different and discussion with the teacher after filling out the forms may reveal that the student has other needs and wants but has trouble expressing them.

However, the course is not set simply after performing a needs analysis but rather dynamically developed with student input at each stage. Hutchinson and Waters (1986) provide a healthy perspective in what they called a learning-centred approach to course design:

a Course design is a negotiated process. There is no single factor which has an outright determining influence on the content of the course. The ESP learning situation and the target situation will both influence the nature of the syllabus, materials, methodology and evaluation procedures. Similarly each of these components will influence and be influenced by the others.

b Course design is a dynamic process. It does not move in a linear fashion from initial analysis to completed course. Needs and resources vary with time. The course design, therefore, needs to have built-in feedback channels to enable the course to respond to developments. (p. 74)

8 How

How addresses the question 'How am I going to teach to attain the desired goals (short term or long term), in the time and place appointed, with this particular person?' It is essentially a pedagogical-procedural question. But in 1/1 it can be extremely interpersonal, i.e. adjusted to the student's and teacher's perception of the task. Chapter 5 is devoted to answering it in part, with a catalogue of ideas that have proved useful in many situations. But the answer is extremely difficult to find without getting answers to your other questions first. For in 1/1, the student should also have a say (most or all of it) as to the **how**. If the student insists that learning grammar rules is the best way for her, then the teacher's job is to help in that direction. However, students may think they learn one way best while simply not knowing about other possibilities.

On the other hand, the needs and desires of the students may not be what the teacher thinks is best, having learned differently herself. This egocentric temptation to generalise should be fought. Learners learn in different ways for different goals. If they have conceptualised what they see as best for them, then it most probably is, at least from the initial motivational point of view. However, part of the teacher's task as an adviser also allows her to suggest alternative ways to learn (see Case History 1). It may take some training and convincing before someone who just wants to be able to read texts will accept activities apparently outside reading as effective, but there is crossover from one skill to another. As Hutchinson and Waters (1986) state, 'The fact that the learner will eventually use the knowledge gained only for reading is largely irrelevant. What is of most concern is how the learner can learn that knowledge most effectively. If the effectiveness of the process can be enriched by the use of other skills, then that is what should be done.' (Hutchinson and Waters 1986: 75)

The teacher may create with the student many of the materials for the specific situation and needs. To give complete lesson plans here would be counter to the principle that the greatest advantage to 1/1 teaching is this ability to tune in to the particular interests and needs of a particular person with particular characteristics in a particular place with a certain amount of time to give, and counter to the idea that to a great extent the student can tell the teacher how he or she wants to learn. Holec (1979) calls this the 'specific personal dimension':

As regards the definition of objectives . . ., self-direction of learning entails some very big differences as compared with the definition made from outside by a teacher or teaching establishment . . . . an objective based essentially on the field of learning, the same for everyone, is replaced by progressive steps (a succession of objectives) of a diverse nature fixed for and by each learner by reference to his personal needs and motivations, progressive steps which may be challenged and amended by the learner at any time. (p. 12)

Tuning in framework for 1/1

In explaining how ESP courses are developed at Colchester English Study Centre, Jonathan Seath (at the 1987 IATEFL Conference) included, in addition to the student input into the five questions above, the need for continual feedback throughout the course and then post-course feedback, weeks or months later. Knowing whether your teaching has had positive results in the real world and how your teaching might have been more useful in the eyes of students and employers can help immensely with later students. Finding out their continuing difficulties, their frustrations, and their joys are eye-opening experiences.

5 Materials, ideas and techniques

■■■■ Chapter 5 surveys materials, ideas and techniques that you can use in 1/1 teaching. Many more can be found in other teacher resource books. Listed here are just some that have worked well. Teachers in continual development will amass many more as their experience grows.

1 Students as primary material

With adult learners 1/1 is seldom an imposed language learning situation. It is usually chosen by the student, and as such is a display of self-directed learning. A pre-constructed course runs counter to this concept since it will have already decided what, in what order, and how the student is to learn. Thus, putting complete language lessons into a book for 1/1 would run counter to the idea that the lesson planning springs from the students, their needs and how they want to learn. Even in ESP, many teachers find the texts on the special topic not specific enough to the actual needs and situations of any given student. This is when the student's own authentic material becomes most useful.

This does not mean that the teacher needs no materials, methodology and planning. On the contrary, a good 1/1 teacher forseeably would need a larger 'bag of tricks' and a wider grasp of different methodologies than the conventional classroom teacher in order to adapt to each student's different needs and desired method of learning. It also does not mean that teachers must master all the specialist fields of their students in order to teach them – an impossibility in any case. 'The acceptance that the learner possesses the specialist knowledge of the content while the tutor has the specialist knowledge of language study techniques can lead to a collaborative approach to learning and help to accelerate the trend towards autonomy' (Dickinson, 1987). In other words, this collaboration helps to create the equal encounter already discussed.

Adrian Underhill (1988) put it well in his article 'Teaching without a coursebook':

I have learnt a lot from using published materials and the accompanying teachers' books, especially in my first years of teaching. At the same time I have also found that materials, especially coursebooks, can come between me and my students, preventing me from directly experiencing and responding to the moment by moment energy and vitality of their own learning experience. If I'm not careful I reduce myself to a 'materials operator', separated from my learners by a screen of 'things to do'.

Underhill believes that the students, with the teacher, can do much of what a textbook writer does in a more relevant fashion. Thus, if they want a dialogue, dictation, or text they write one; if they want a picture they draw one; if they want an exercise they construct one; if they want a tape they make one, etc.

The key to planning lessons in 1/1 is looking at each individual student and soliciting their input as to **what** and **how**. This implies not only doing a needs-analysis but a how-analysis with the student (Allwright 1982).

In the sections that follow are a few general ideas concerning possible materials and techniques that have worked in many, although certainly not all, 1/1 encounters. They are not detailed lesson plans but rather a smorgasbord of ideas that may or may not work depending on the student's and the teacher's abilities to adapt them to their specific uses.

Keep in mind that this discussion of materials is two sided: there are 1 materials for the teacher that provide options for exercises and activities to use with the student, and there are 2 materials already designed for the student's direct use. The trend, I believe, (at least in private instruction) is for more of the first type of materials. This is a reflection of the often unconscious realisation of teachers that they need ideas to adapt to their situations, not explicit lesson plans, and this is the reason that there has been a very popular explosion of teacher resource books which provide different ways to use students as the primary material in any teaching situation.

In the next few sections, I first comment on different types of materials (commercial, authentic, concrete, student- and teacher-made) and suggest the creation of situationally motivated teacher- and student-produced materials. Then various general activities and ideas are presented for your consideration.

2 Commercial ELT materials

Much of what is already done in mainstream language teaching can be used by the 1/1 teacher. The wealth of materials is practically endless, however their applicability to any one person in the form in which they exist is usually small. In other words, the 1/1 teacher can and should tap the immense amount of resources available, but at the same time realise that they often can only be used in part, and most need to be adapted in order to be intensely relevant to any one student (see Stevick, 1971). Bowen and Madsen (1978) take it for granted that 'it is necessary to particularise teaching materials in a classroom; this is the heart of teaching and should be a prominent concern in any teacher-training course' (p. vii).

Teachers who have told me they use a course book say they also appreciate the flexibility in 1/1 which allows them to pull resources and ideas from many areas. Considering the diversity of students, it's a good idea to have a well-stocked library of EFL 'idea books', or have access to them. Several of these books (not all specially made for ELT) are listed in the References. A textbook can be reassuring for many students, while for others it can be an unwanted obligation. Each teacher has to decide with the students what is best for them.

The field of English for Special Purposes has already narrowed down the audience somewhat with books prepared for business English, the sciences, and for many professions. Good texts also exist for students wanting to improve reading comprehension, composition skills, etc. However, these books are usually not intensely relevant for any one person because they are trying to be relevant to as many people as possible, or at best a category of people. The teacher can use them as they are, but, more often than not, they will work much better if they are adjusted to her student's specific needs, levels, and interests, making them maximally efficient.

At the same time, I feel materials should not dominate: 1/1 means one *person* to one *person*, and this intensely people-centred interaction is one of its most appealing features. When beginning, especially, teachers feel more secure having a lot of materials. Handouts are concrete referents which can take the attention away from the teacher at uncertain first encounters. However, the danger is in continually hiding behind materials instead of developing the social interpersonal side of teaching 1/1. In order for the student to receive quality time with the teacher, textbook tasks which don't actually require the teacher's presence can be done at other times than that spent with the teacher.

3 Authentic materials

In addition to published ELT materials, a plethora of authentic material exists which teachers can find or get from their students. Ask your students to bring you copies of documents that they work with in English, brochures they have, training manuals, and correspondence. Once you know who your students are, you can begin collecting possible materials from magazines, newspapers, and other sources. (In fact, it's as if you can't avoid them – you find your students in everything you read!)

These materials may be used in a lesson, given to the students to read on their own, or sent with a short note (see mail, page 73). Depending on the level of the student and interest in the particular topic, such materials may be exploited completely or only in passing to bring out the use of a few terms or to reinforce something that was discussed.

For bankers, I often take short articles concerning the economy out of *Time* and *Newsweek* and ask the student to explain a few concepts to me. If my questions solicit an area of little concern with my student I let it drop. Other times students spend several hours explaining the background and working of the different phenomena. These different reactions to different materials are due in part to the materials but much more to the individual characteristics of students. That is why it is so important to be continually open to adjusting to the student and to ignore material if need be (no matter how good it was with other students or how much time you spent finding and preparing it).

4 Concrete referents

Concrete referents are actual objects to hold on to, to use and talk about. They help to give otherwise abstract language an immediate reference. They help to provide comprehensible input (Krashen, 1985). These may be anything from the actual products of a company to soft balls and cuisenaire rods, model ships to the family photo album. Especially for students at beginning levels where speaking about the here and now is easier, having concrete referents to refer to is a great aid (see Krashen and Terrell, 1983). Of course the choice of actually doing something during a lesson (e.g. visiting a museum, baking a cake, or skiing) presents its own natural concrete referents.

5 Adapting and creating materials

As we suggested above, many of the commercial materials or authentic materials will be improved by a bit of adapting. The teacher can take good ideas and apply them to the particular situations of the students, taking into account their interests and levels. There is actually a continuum between using a text directly and the individual creation of materials, with many intermediate possibilities from simply changing place names to restructuring the whole content (Murphey, 1985a). Teachers notice after a while that individual materials they have prepared for other students can seldom be used, without changing them somewhat, for another student because they have become very personalised. The ideas and techniques can be used again, but, for them to be intensely relevant, they may need to be adjusted to each student either in how they are written or how they are used. Far from being a disadvantage, this keeps teachers on their toes and keeps them from stagnating into always repeating the same things instead of showing students by example how to adjust while communicating.

6 The individual textbook

Teachers normally amass dozens of files of handouts that they have produced and adapted to work in their particular situation. In 1979, I proposed that those were essentially the raw materials that authors used to create textbooks and that teachers could do the same, creating texts for their own particular situation. Wilberg (1987) carries this one step further, proposing that the teacher and student in 1/1 create a personalised file that becomes the student's 'text' and becomes a record of the course. The individualised textbook also becomes a valuable resource for the student in the future.

One of the main purposes of a textbook in a conventional course is that it acts as a kind of concrete referent, i.e. the students and teacher can say, 'this text is the English Course' and there is a kind of psychological security in that. Many students in 1/1 will want to have a text for such reasons. If they can be patient and watch their own personalised text grow from lesson to lesson, it is much more rewarding.

7 First classes

Typically first classes are organisational and centre on getting to know each other so that you are comfortable working together. The teacher needs to be prepared to direct the student to the goal of serious work, but at the same time needs to be open to let the student take as much responsibility as he or she wishes (see self-directed learning page 71). The teacher tries to respond to the needs, desires, and goals of the student in order to create a rapport capable of stimulating the greatest acquisition. Typical first class activities are:

- Completing a personal profile form and needs/goals list so the teacher understands better the student's background and what the student wants from the meetings (see example page 60).
- Orally expanding on this questionnaire and following the lead of the student.
- The teacher giving the same kind of personal information using the same language (see 'mirroring' page 67).
- Setting of procedures. For example, with someone who needs improvement with telephone English, I may decide with her that I will call three times a week and ask for different information in English. I will record the calls and exploit them in the next class. But first the student needs to tell me what kind of information people are liable to ask her for. For another student, we may decide to exchange letters.

The last ten minutes of an hour's lesson, the notes that I will have taken are reviewed. The tone shifts a bit as we decide implicitly that now we are going to look at the form of what was said. The message is, 'I understood everything very well and enjoyed it. Here are just a few points that you may want to consider' (see example page 65).

The first class especially should end on a positive note, hopefully with a task that is easy and amusing, and with the student leaving with a positive impression of the encounter and what future ones will be like. This may be a relevant comic strip or an amusing article that I will briefly give the background and content of and then leave with the student.

8 Class planning

I find myself usually going to each lesson with three times as many activities and ideas to exploit as are possible in the time given. That way if for some reason we finish certain things very quickly, or the student really isn't in the mood for certain types of activities, I can adjust and switch to something else. Having a large menu of possible activities, topics, and exercises allows the teacher to be much more adjustable than would ever be possible with a group of students. The trick is to tune in to the student upon arrival, and throughout the lesson, and decide what would work best at any moment. It also gives an intensive feel to the meetings because there are so many things I want to do with the student, find out about, and tell her about.

In planning classes, try to recapitulate what was done in the preceding one, or reuse some of the same material in order to refresh the student's memory and give some cohesion to the set of lessons. After each class, I usually note down what we actually did, as a kind of post-class syllabus so I can start the next class with a reminder of the previous class and choose materials accordingly. I attempt to bring in some grammar or vocabulary point through the use of either an exercise or article, and I will list a series of topics to discuss and questions I want to ask about each. These topics are usually questions about the student's work, interests, or something that we've talked about and I know there is interest in. The daily newspaper often provides me with recent topics relevant to the student and which the student may also have just read about. The English class takes on added value when current concerns are discussed as opposed to history (history is always there and what is happening now will soon be history – catch it while it's exciting and it's much more efficient as language learning material). I always try to have something to actually give the student to take away. This may be a handout exercise, an article, the loan of a book or music cassette.

9 Personal profiles

The purpose of the personal profile is to gather information about the student which can be used to get to know the student, as material to exploit later, as a basis for selection of other material, and also as something to talk about during the first lesson. The student can fill out the profile beforehand or during the first lesson. It can be exploited orally as well, with the teacher asking questions for clarification and expansion concerning different points. If the student is already strong enough verbally, the teacher may wish to ask the student the questions and fill it in herself so that there is more immediate interaction. Usually the personal profile, like the curriculum vitae, offers a lot of opportunities to recognise the student's positive achievements and strong points. Also the topic of discussion is definitely well known to the student. These two points help to counterbalance the 'speaking a foreign language' effect and the first class jitters. If they are up to it, I can also ask them to fill one out for me, asking the same questions that I just asked of them.

Personal Profile

(feel free to leave anything blank)

Attach C.V. please. Please feel free to attach more on another sheet and to add any typical documents that you must work with in English.

Full name: _____

Address: _____

Home phone: _____

Profession: _____

Address: _____

Business phone: _____

Age: _____

Family status (children): _____

Professional goals: _____

Sports interests: _____

Musical preferences: _____

Other hobbies: _____

Native language(s): _____

Other languages spoken or read: _____

English background: In schools? _____
In an English–speaking country? _____

Present level of English: _____

What do you need English for? (exams, travel, academic, business, science, etc.) _____

What must you do with English? speak (teach, explain, argue, sell, present papers, chair meetings, advise, introduce people, negotiate, buy, cocktail party, talk on the telephone), write (letters, reports, telexes), listen (to lectures, radio, television), read (reports, newspapers, manuals, textbooks, letters)...

_____
_____
_____
_____

Who are some of the people you will be interacting with?

_____
_____
_____
_____

What are some of the things they are liable to do? ask for information, criticise, question, try to persuade you, teach you, negotiate, etc.

_____
_____
_____
_____

What are some of the things you must say?

_____
_____
_____
_____

What do you think is the best way for me to help you? (What do you want to do during our lessons?)

_____
_____
_____
_____
_____

Write one of your favourite sayings (in any language).

_____
_____
_____
_____

Thankyou.

10 Questionnaires and agendas

The best thing about questionnaires in 1/1 (like the personal profile) is that they are usually 100 per cent egocentric. The student is on-line all the time. First, this means that the student knows the information and the teacher doesn't. The student is never wrong. Secondly, they are very interested in the topic. (That is the reason so many magazines have tests and questionnaires that readers fill in and find out how stressed, sexed, healthy, intelligent, or whatever, they are. Grab the readers' egos and you've got them hooked.)

Questionnaires

Using different types of questionnaires allows the teacher to gather more information to be used later in planning lessons. They also spark much discussion not only about the topics covered in them but about their reliability in general. The following example concerns musical tastes and habits.

What music do you speak?

1 Age _____

2 Sex _____

3 Native language _____

    Other languages spoken _____

Tick (✓) if your answer is 'yes'.

4 _____ I play an instrument. Which one(s)? _____

5 _____ I sing in a choir.

6 _____ I read music.

7 _____ I sing in the shower.

8 _____ I wake up to music.

9 _____ I go to sleep with music.

10 _____ I study with music.

11 _____ I play/played in a band.

12 _____ I take dance classes. What kind? _____

13 _____ I do aerobics.

14 _____ I have written a song(s).

15 _____ I read music magazines. Which ones? _____

Give approximate answers in minutes and/or hours per day.

16 I listen to music on the radio for about _____

17 I listen to cassettes/CDs/LPs for about _____

18 I watch music videos on TV for about _____

19 I watch other programmes on TV for about _____

20 What percentage (approximately) of the songs that you listen to are:

instruments _____% in English _____% in other languages _____%

Tick (✓) which answer is true for you.

21 Do you play the same song several times in succession?

never _____ sometimes _____ often _____ very often _____

22 Do you choose music according to your activity?

never _____ sometimes _____ often _____ very often _____

23 Do you use music just for background?

never _____ sometimes _____ often _____ very often _____

24 Do you listen to classical music?

never _____ sometimes _____ often _____ very often _____

25 Does music ever disturb you?

never _____ sometimes _____ often _____ very often _____

26 On the back list your three favourite groups or singers at the moment (the one you like most first), your favourite song at the moment, and which artists you find most attractive visually. Thank you.

Questionnaires can be constructed by you or your students, or taken from magazines, books and newspapers. In addition to the personal profile, teachers may be interested in gathering information as to their students' work and study habits (past and present), their beliefs about the nature of language and the language learning process, how they think they learn best, their reaction to stress, and their strong and weak points in their native languages. Again, a more interactively verbal way to use a questionnaire is for the teacher to fill it out for the student while asking the questions, and then to have the student fill out a form for the teacher while asking the questions.

Among EFL materials, questionnaires can be found in Moscowitz (1978), Porter Ladousse (1983), and Klippel (1984). Simon *et al.* (1972) have a wide array of intriguing questions and questionnaires for values clarification. The humanistic activities can be easily adjusted to the 1/1 situation, and changed somewhat for the student who may find them overly personal.

Agendas

A regular activity with many of my students is going over agendas. I ask them to open their agenda and tell me what they have done since our last meeting (practising the past tenses), or what they have planned for the forthcoming week (future). Depending on their level, a vocabulary list with verbs, in present and past, may be reviewed first and I might tell them what my week was like as an example.

The routine day might be handled in a similar fashion. Conditional forms can be practised also using the agenda: 'If you had not gone to Germany on Wednesday, what would you have done? If you were at the office now what would you be doing? If your committee meeting is cancelled what will you do?' A favourite of many is setting up their ideal agenda for a week (which usually includes a conference in the Bahamas or entertaining a client in a ski resort).

11 Note-taking sheet: the class record

A handy technique, as already mentioned in the case histories, is simply having a piece of paper beside the teacher. Not only does it add a bit of psychological schoolishness that many students need, but it is useful methodologically, for the teacher, and acquisitionally for the student. At the top of the sheet you might note the major points that you hope to go over during the lesson. During the lesson you use it as a buffer zone between corrections and the student. Instead of correcting mispronunciations immediately, or interrupting to explain a grammar point or a vocabulary item, you can quickly and discreetly jot down a few words so that you can explain them later (as well as simultaneously giving correct reformulations if possible). This has the advantage of **1** not interrupting the flow and struggle of meaning-making and **2** of softening the impact of negative error correction. During the last part of the lesson, or at a moment that presents itself well, these things can be explained, preferably recalling the original context.

You might also note down some interesting ideas that you think might be expanded on or a grammatical pattern that the student is using naturally well so that you can later compliment her on it. Taking notes of the positive as well as the erroneous points helps to make the encounter more positive. Students may not realise that they used a difficult word correctly or that the way they phrased an idea was well done. It gives them more confidence when you let them know.

This sheet also gathers vocabulary and diagrams as the lesson unfolds and becomes a record of what went on. As mentioned already, the notes are extremely useful with some, however not with all. Part of adjusting appropriately is figuring out what techniques work well with which students, and being well enough prepared and courageous enough to try something else when things aren't working well.

Below is a reproduction of one of these sheets (a remembered approximation, as students always take them away with them):

Mr Historian : Monday evening 19h. December 1987. Restaurant.

*A Fall of the $. 1929 Crash. Tokyo next? Impact on Switzerland?
Up-coming elections in U.S.
agenda, last month, next month.*

Student	Me (explaining afterwards)
B 1 many works	count (1, 2, 3, 4 ...) many projects non-count much work
2 actually	(false friends) -- really, xxx presently
3 19--87, 1987, etc.	'19 hundred 87,' or simply '1987'
4 craXch	Crash-sh
5 got too big	'blown out of proportion' exaggeration
6 contageux	ious
7 months clothes	(close) don't have to pronounce the 'th'
8 watchId ed (t)	ed ch, k, s, p =(t) after voiceless g, z, b = (d) after voiced d, t = (id) after (d) or (t)
9 incomparable	incompàrable
10 impossible to win	'catch 22' - vicious circle - a no-win situation
11 'When will we see us again?'	each other

Because your students take away the note sheet after each lesson, it is helpful to keep a notebook to write in as soon as possible after the lesson to remind yourself what you went over, new words, and problems covered. Then you can refer to this before the next lesson and start off referring to items from the last time and the things that were done, reinforcing them and providing the student with a familiar framework to begin the new lesson. Some teachers also keep very organised files for each student.

12 Listening and eye contact

'A good listener has magic! A good listener has the ability to make people feel good, and is as valuable at a party as a good talker. But just listening isn't enough. One should listen intelligently by trying to find out what the other person would really like to communicate.' (Wright, 1987: 58)

My retired executive student, Mlle Flandres, teaches me a lot about listening. She says that her bosses always sent her to lunch with the big clients they were trying to sell to. Most were men and they loved being listened to and being understood. She had developed the ability of knowing how to ask questions and showing interest. Sometimes she felt guilty for pretending attention, she admits, but most of the time she really was learning a lot. Even with the not so interesting, she was learning what they liked and didn't like, how they saw the world, and about human nature in general.

Tennis player/coach Gallwey (1974) tells a story of being asked an intriguing question: 'If a wise man and a fool talk to each other, who will learn the most?' Gallwey at first reasoned, as many of us would, that since the wise man knows so much, the fool would learn more since he has so much to learn. Then after letting it sink in a bit more he realised that the wise man is probably wise because he has learned how to learn. The fool is a fool because he doesn't know how. The wise man, if he is truly wise, should be able to learn in any situation. Then, Gallwey reasoned, he should be learning as much on the tennis court during his lessons as his students, or he was perhaps a fool. So he began trying to learn about his students, how they learned, how they reacted to different instructions, and to no instructions. He studied letting them just feel good and the impact of positive and negative feedback, how they formed habits, broke habits, and what their frustration did to their bodies. He realised he had an enormous amount of things to learn from them. Of course this was also the basic strategy of Mlle Flandres with her clients. This does not imply that our students are fools, but it does imply that we as teachers may have fossilised our wisdom into foolishness if we think we have nothing to learn from them.

Teacher listening, then, plays several roles: it gives students on-line practice in generating language, it gives the teacher input (content, linguistic, and affective) which needs to be adjusted and reacted to (learned from), it tells the student that she has something valuable to share and thus raises confidence (equalising the encounter). '... if you would like to be a good conversationalist, be an attentive listener. Encourage others to talk about themselves. To be interesting, be interested. Ask questions that other people will enjoy answering. Encourage them to talk about themselves and what they have done.' (Wright, 1987:57)

One of the keys to showing attentiveness is eye contact, which varies from one culture to another. In most western countries, when your eyes are focused on the speaker's eyes, it tells the speaker that you are with them. If your eyes are elsewhere or if they can't see you, they may not be very sure. A friend of mine who manages a large staff, and who is continually being asked questions, has his desk so that his back is to his open door. When someone pokes their head in quickly to ask a question he usually doesn't turn around. They can't see his eyes and don't know his immediate reaction. The longer he pauses the more insecure the asker usually is. The asker also feels uncomfortable asking more or explaining more to someone's back. Although at the limit of being rude, it's a powerful position when others don't know your immediate reaction and must wait for it. Actually he's a nice chap, but being often asked to take decisions and resolve problems, he probably has unconsciously reasoned that 'the less they see of the window of my soul, the more I can control.' Taking our eyes elsewhere for too long when someone is talking to us is to say we are uninterested. Keeping them glued to the speaker is to say we are very interested, please continue. The speaker can then concentrate on the message and not be preoccupied by negative affective messages.

Of course lovers know that all they need are each other's eyes. Words often only seem to get in the way. I don't suggest that you communicate infatuation to your clients, but it is something close to it when you are giving them all your attention through intense eye encouragement.

13 Mirroring

Mirroring behaviour is basically a technique to build rapport by tuning into and, to a certain extent, imitating your partner's behaviour. The idea here is that 100 per cent of your attention is focused on your partner and her efforts at communication. Bandler and Grinder (1979:55) call this 'up-time'. During this time one tries to match one's partner physically, affectively, intellectually, and linguistically, in a sense becoming the other person so it is easier to understand what is being said. They call this pacing. This may mean assuming similar postures, eye contact, and even breathing; attempting to feel the emotions that the other person manifests or talks about; speaking about the same things as your partner in a non-judgemental fashion (e.g. not being condescending about pop music when speaking to an adolescent); using the same vocabulary, length of sentences, rate and loudness of speech, with the same intensity and intonation. This should not be taken as 'aping' someone to the point of ridicule. It is simply sympathising as much as possible.

As stated above, the goal of mirroring, or pacing, is to build rapport. This is a necessary first step if someone like a teacher wants to then 'lead' someone somewhere. Once rapport is established, it is as if your partner has accepted you as a non-threatening extension of herself, and then she will accept also being led. For a 1/1 teacher this leading is in the form of linguistic reformulation of faulty phrases, suggesting activities, and giving advice. Of course this can even entail a healthy measure of disagreement within a situation of rapport (see 'cognitive conflict', page 100).

Mirroring and leading may be negatively called 'manipulation', which one could argue is the goal of most education in the first place – to convince students that certain things should be known, or have value, over other things. If students agree to this sort of manipulation there is rarely any problem. If they disagree, education becomes forced and is exceedingly difficult for student and teacher. A 1/1 student who comes voluntarily has chosen to learn and to be led, but at times may have other barriers or show resistance. Mirroring can help overcome these problems and also tune a teacher into what and how to teach best to each individual.

Mirroring and leading are of course not new and examples can often be found in literature. Charles Dickens provides an example of mirroring/manipulation/leading, which in this case uses flattery and charm. Rachael, a spinster aunt, joins a prospective lover/husband in at first admiring her younger nieces who may be more appealing to him than she is, and then leads him to different conclusions:

'Do you think my nieces pretty?' whispered their affectionate aunt to Mr Tupman.
'I should, if their aunt wasn't here,' replied the ready Pickwickian, with a passionate glance.
'Oh, you naughty man – but really, if their complexions were a little, *little* better, don't you think they would be nice-looking girls – by candle-light?'
'Yes, I think they would,' said Mr Tupman, with an air of indifference.
'Oh, you quiz – I know what you were going to say.'
'What?' inquired Mr Tupman, who had not precisely made up his mind to say anything at all.
'You were going to say that Isabel stoops – I know you were – you men are such observers. Well, so she does; it can't be denied; and certainly, if there is one thing more than another that makes a girl look ugly, it is stooping. I often tell her, that when she gets a little older, she'll be quite frightful. Well, you *are* a quiz!'
Mr Tupman had no objection to earning the reputation at so cheap a rate: so he looked very knowing, and smiled mysteriously.
'What a sarcastic smile,' said the admiring Rachael: 'I declare I'm quite afraid of you.'
'Afraid of me!'
'Oh, you can't disguise anything from me – I know what that smile means, very well.'
'What?' said Mr Tupman, who had not the slightest notion himself.
'You mean,' said the amiable aunt, sinking her voice still lower –
'You mean, that you don't think Isabella's stooping is as bad as Emily's boldness. Well, she *is* bold! You cannot think how wretched it makes me sometimes. I'm sure I cry about it for hours together – my dear brother is so good, and so unsuspicious, that he never sees it; if he did, I'm quite certain it

would break his heart. I wish I could think it was only manner – I hope it may be – ' (Here the affectionate relative heaved a deep sigh, and shook her head despondingly.)
(from *The Posthumous Papers of the Pickwick Club*)

Tom Sawyer was of course also an excellent pedagogue in convincing his friends about the fun/prestige/value of white-washing a fence. First, he had to make them give up their illusion that he wasn't enjoying it himself, then induce a desire in them to accompany him. The fact that he was able to gradually elevate white-washing to such a height allowed him even to be paid for letting others do his work! The interesting thing was that the others really did enjoy it because they had completely joined his fabricated reality. One might even wonder if Tom himself didn't regret not doing more of the work when he saw how popular it became, or at least he might have asked more in exchange for the privilege. (For an extremely interesting analysis of these two passages, and others, see de Beaugrande and Dressler, 1981)

Of course I am not advocating manipulation; however, charm is a part of rapport, and we cannot deny that it is used manipulatively at times. To refuse to build this rapport because it might become manipulative would not get us anywhere. Rather we should strive to make a foundation upon which the healthy negotiation of goals, materials and method can evolve. If the rapport is mature, then both parties actually lead mutually. In 1/1, as opposed to much group teaching, the teacher can allow the student to provide the content and direction whenever possible; the teacher provides principally the form, control and stimulation for further content exploration by the student.

Actually this is what happens a great part of the time with small children learning to talk. Most adults will stoop down and quickly assume the emotions of a child partner, use the child's language as they accept any topics brought up, imitate the child's intonation, and play in 'their world' first. However, caretakers, and teachers, are not content always to give the same messages (see Brown, 1977). They adjust only as far as they need to in order to make themselves understood. Thus, they are continually providing sequences which contain language just beyond the child's current level, pulling the child progressively toward more complex forms and ideas.

Some people mirror instinctively all the time, others do so when they want to. In lay language this is often referred to as having a persuasive character, or a lot of charm. I believe teachers can consciously improve their ability to do this consistently.

14 Action language

Only linguists and teachers spend most of their time talking about language, meta communicating. Normal people do other things with it. Especially low level students can be helped by combining our social interaction with physical action: by baking a cake, visiting a museum, playing tennis, going skiing, or having a tour of someone's factory, for example. Encourage your students to do something with you and you've got a task which is natural to talk about. This is similar to the use of Total Physical Response, or TPR (Asher, 1977) in classroom teaching where the students do actions and tasks physically. This corresponds also to using concrete referents and to language learning through dealing with subject matter, what Krashen (1985) calls in the school environment 'sheltered courses'. Inherent in both ideas is that comprehension usually precedes the ability to produce, not only at beginning stages but with later acquisition as well.

Subject matter teaching, also referred to as content-based instruction, has become a necessity in the U.S. in the last fifteen years. With the last wave of immigration, the government was faced with the huge task of integrating the new immigrants into the work force and schools. The authorities found out they could not afford to teach them conventionally for years, there were just too many and they were forced to give these new immigrants survival skills like how to telephone, take a bus, and interview for a job with English as the medium. (Crandal, speaking at the 1988 IATEFL Conference) They found content instruction also had the immigrants acquiring the language faster. The irony is that in public schools, where survival is not the problem, we can afford to be inefficient in our language teaching; we've got time and money and no great pressing need. If we want to beat the old adage 'Success breeds mediocrity', then we need to find out what the specific motivating needs of our students are. If these needs can't be found then perhaps we shouldn't be teaching, because our teaching will most likely be inefficient.

Having taught numerous summer courses to children, I find the games and physical activities provide many more opportunities for language learning than keeping them sitting at a desk (see Allwright concerning learning opportunities 1984a and b). We might say that having fun is the special purpose of childhood. It is one of a child's primary motivations for doing anything. I recently read a brochure on Pilgrims (England) 'Language in Action' programmes for children that seem to be built around the same principle. I've also seen several advertisements by language schools offering a skiing–language learning weekend. Some holiday sports centres are now offering language courses in conjunction with sports lessons. Hopefully, they are combining the two to make the language learning more natural.

Like any other lesson, action and content lessons require preparation stages which may include developing a vocabulary and idioms list and setting goals before doing it (e.g. we are going to practise giving instructions, commenting on art, etc.) It may take a bit of thought as to how you will plan talk time in activities which normally present little. Such activities as fishing and sailing present plenty of talk time. Skiing also provides natural pauses (riding the lifts up or after a fall). But activities like tennis require some forethought to practise a bit more language. If I am a much better tennis player, I may give a lesson which is like Total Physical

Response, in which body movement accompanies words to make them clear. If my partner is as good as I am, we risk just playing tennis and not saying much. Two ways around this are **1** playing doubles in which the proximity of your student will improve the amount of communication, or **2** pretend you are left handed (if you're right handed) and take a lesson from your student. If a way can't be found then the activity should not count as a lesson. It doesn't mean you can't do it, it just means that the lesson may be during the dinner afterwards.

Subject matter teaching is basically what happens in immersion programmes in Canada. Students learn French as a by-product of learning other things. As Krashen says, 'Subject matter teaching, when it's made comprehensible, is language teaching' (BBC Film *A Child's Guide to Language Learning*). Thus learning about banking or art in English, whether the student is teaching the teacher or the teacher the student, means that both are concentrating on the information, the message, not on the form, and the proper effort will be made to adjust so that the communication is successful. People learn a language for what they can do with it, and they learn a language by doing something positive with it. Sharing information and ideas of high interest is highly motivating. Discussing grammar may be interesting subject matter to many teachers but seldom is to students.

15 Advising and self-directed learning

As noted in the case histories, the teacher can be a very valuable adviser to students, not only about where to go for a linguistic holiday, but about how to shape their present environment to make it more conducive to acquiring the skills they desire in the language. Assuming you are teaching adults, their choice to have lessons with you already means they are self-directed. When they are away from you they can continue to learn, but it may very well be that they need guidance in exactly how they can do this, and the choices that they have available in controlling their own learning. The fact that you can give this guidance means that your worth as a teacher reaches far beyond the hours that you may meet with your students.

An excellent book on the topic is Dickinson's (1987) *Self-instruction in Language Learning* (see also IATEFL's special interest group for Learner Independence). Self-instruction or learner independence holds as a general educational goal the building of autonomy in learning, but it doesn't mean that students simply work alone and the teacher is redundant. On the contrary, it means that students learn to take gradually more and more responsibility for the choices of what and how they learn, which may ultimately be with a teacher. The teacher is used as a resource and a guide (a valued consultant, in business terms) who can give relevant 1/1 attention in a classroom or programme where students are semi-autonomously working towards their individual goals through self-selected materials that they find relevant to their needs.

Little did I know that I was practising semi-autonomous and autonomous learning methodology before reading Dickinson's book, but I was of course. Teachers all over the world are doing wonderful things that academics one day give names to. The naming is good in that it makes these wonderful things accessible to more teachers. But it doesn't mean that you are not a good teacher if you are not doing something named by academia. It just means they haven't yet found a name for your 'wonderfulnesses'. If it works, do it. Don't wait for a name.

The raison d'être of self-instruction is much the same as with 1/1: to account for individual differences among learners and their aims. In most group work when everyone hears and does the same thing, individual learning efficiency may be reduced. It is clear that when the learners and their individual goals are given complete attention, motivation also improves. A personal example is that I have never freely worked so hard in my life as I have on my PhD, because I chose the topic and the perspective. I have often thought that if allowed to do mini-PhDs when a child, my education would have been immensely more valuable. On top of that, it's fun. School seldom was. My advisers have to adapt themselves to my choice of topic and our 1/1 sessions are extremely fruitful. The philosophy behind, and the practice of self-instruction are harmonious complements to 1/1 instruction (see Holec, 1979).

Of course advising students how to improve their extra-class contact can also be done with school age students. It's just that the motivation is often not as strong as with adults. However, telling them about special programmes on T.V. in English (interviews with pop stars, concerts, etc.) and providing optional reading material concerning their interests (sports, fashion, etc.) can have them involved with little regard to what language it might be in.

Teachers adjusting perspectives

As stated above, teachers traditionally have decided the what and the how of language learning, thinking that they know the students' present knowledge, their needs, and how they can learn most efficiently. Self-instruction questions these beliefs, and rightly so. Melody Noll's exercise on the following page is an excellent example of just how a teacher can miscalculate and is a good sensitising exercise to try with your students.

I once chose a text for a student and was at a loss for a vocabulary exercise to do with it. So I tried an experiment. I asked the student to read the article and make the following lists:

1 Words I recognise but don't really know.

2 Words I absolutely don't know and can't figure out from the context.

3 Words I should know.

4 Words I think a teacher would choose for me to learn.

At the same time, I wrote down what I imagined she would put in her lists. **My list and her list had practically nothing in common!** My number 4 items shocked her: 'What? You thought I didn't know what *that* word meant?!', and her number 2 items were an eye-opener for me as I said to myself 'What? You don't even know that Mickey Mouse expression?'

The point is that we perhaps should let students contribute more to their own learning instead of doing so much faulty guesswork ourselves.

16 Distance contact with the teacher

Two communicative tasks for students away from the teacher involve the mail and telephone.

a **Mail** You can often write to your students in the target language, sending them articles or commenting on something seen or heard that may concern them. This may be an article on economic trends, or on a concert that came up in conversation, or simply to say hello. Sometimes I even send cartoons that I like from the newspaper. It's amazing how much they in turn write to me. Other 1/1 teachers have told me they get their students to exchange letters with their families and friends as well. You can also provide addresses where they can write to ask for free information (embassies, travel bureaux, tourist offices, etc.)

b **Telephone** Calling to set or confirm appointments adds another dimension to your repertoire of authentic teaching techniques. A successful call of even a few minutes in a foreign language can be an intense affair for most students. Telephone-English, a new trend that is catching on fast, proposes whole courses on the telephone. Teachers may call for several minutes several times a day to speak English to their clients over the phone as part of a regular paid programme. This type of communication is especially good for those who do a lot of business by phone. But it can be extremely difficult and uncomfortable if not done properly. When we speak we depend a lot on the environmental clues that are around us and the visual messages that contribute to the total message. Telephoning can be discouraging because of the lack of feedback coming from our partner. (Have you ever tried smiling into a telephone and waiting for the response?) Before undertaking a telephone course, the teacher should firmly evaluate the student's ability and needs in order to avoid frustration as much as possible. Another way to use the phone is in giving simple homework assignments:

- Call up an English-speaking embassy and ask for information and documents concerning certain topics (travel abroad, free English learning materials, etc.)

- Call up English-speaking friends of mine, e.g. 'Tim Murphey mentioned to me that you taught Cambridge First Certificate, that you were a good teacher, and I was wondering when your next course began.'

- Call up the local tourist office and speak English, say you are Swedish (thus don't know French and German) if you like, ask for information about the next concert, football match, etc.

- Call up the English department at the university and ask if they have information concerning language courses in English-speaking countries. If yes, when could you come to look at it and perhaps get their advice?

Finally, if you have a telephone recorder you can leave messages for students and record their messages. You can create interesting pseudo-dictations and assignments for your students, something along the lines of:

Hello [a segment of Lionel Richie's song 'Hello'] I just called to say . . . [Stevie Wonder's song] Don't you hate recordings? Me too. Don't worry, you don't have to record anything. From April 2nd to the 17th I'll be away at a conference in Edinburgh. If you would like to write to me there, my address is Tim Murphey, c/o the Café Royal, Arthur's Seat 7, Edinburgh EH9 2JG, or call and leave a message if it's urgent. The number is 031 667 00 77. I'll be back late on the 17th; on the 18th I'll be at my university number all morning 21 31 81. I look forward to speaking with you and please do forgive this recording. It's an inhuman form of communication and will explode when you hear the 'beep' . . . [silence for a few seconds, then a whispered 'boom']

or:

Sorry I'm not at home right now and you have to listen to a stupid recording. The best time to reach me is mornings from 8 to 10. Feel free to leave a message after the inhuman beep, or simply to hang up. 1/1 students please leave time and date of call and confirm our next meeting, time and place. Have a nice day. 'beep'.

Students can take down messages as dictations, record their own appropriate messages, or follow any set of directions you wish to give. Recorded tapes and dictations can then be used at the next meeting.

17 Journals and homework

Two more semi-autonomous tasks are **journals** and, simply, **homework**. Journals seem to be another technique which some students embrace and find extremely useful while others dislike it. The latter group should not be forced. It's an activity that you can suggest they try out and if they dislike it they can stop. I usually give them the following instructions:

THE ENGLISH JOURNAL

The idea behind this journal is that you write something in it every day, for at least a few minutes. You are completely at liberty as to what you write. It can be about what you have done that day, your plans for tomorrow, poetry, a story, complaints, how difficult English is, fantasy, etc. I will collect your journal periodically and read it, or you can choose to keep it private. The ideas are yours and you are completely free to say what you please. If you have a question or ask for a comment I will respond. Try, as much as possible, to incorporate the new words and expressions that you are learning into your writing. Play with the language, and don't only write what you know is correct. Experiment. If you are doubtful about how to use a word, try it!

Always having a fixed time to write is a good idea. Some students do this just before going to bed at night with some soft music in the background. They find that their mind then works on the English during the night. Have fun. ■■■■

Although the journal is a good idea, even the most motivated will usually give it up if they don't receive the feedback necessary to make it rewarding. Little positive comments and questions at the end of the entries can stimulate a student immensely to carry on. And even occasionally writing a full page reaction will show the student that you are involved in the work as well.

Homework, of course, has always been at least semi-autonomous, conducted without the teacher, although perhaps with fellow students and then perhaps covered later in class. I find it wise to ask students explicitly if they want homework or not, so that there is no misunderstanding over what they expect. Some are very serious and want a lot, while others say they want it, then never do it. As a teacher, I never count on going over their homework during the next lesson. If they did it and want to go over it, fine. If not, that's OK, too. Becoming an authoritarian would upset the attempt to balance the encounter. Even when tutoring children, it seems they do more homework subsequently when I say nothing about their negligence. They appreciate me treating them almost as an equal, not trying to send them on a guilt trip, and having a good time during the lesson. I also try to make their homework as authentic as possible. In addition to the regular types of exercises teachers might give (e.g. readings, grammar and vocabulary exercises), some of the more authentic possibilities are:

- write a letter to an Anglo-American company, an author, professor, member of my family, magazine, etc.
- watch a T.V. programme on an English channel and report on it in the next lesson.
- listen to (and perhaps tape) the hit parade from an English speaking radio station and note the top ten (dictation). (See also telephoning.)
- write a summary of the most interesting story (to them) in the international English newspaper, or in the local newspaper (translate).

We can also provide them with the possibility of being completely autonomous with no comeback from the teacher when we give them articles to read and lend them books and cassettes of interviews and music.

18 Personal start-up conversational topics

The following is a brainstorming list of topics and starter questions. Some may even serve as topics for practice in giving presentations, while others may be uninteresting to certain students. These are merely possible starting points that will naturally be expanded upon in conversation. You can think of many more questions to go along with them if you try. The goal is to keep the student at the centre of the content of communication and to use your skills as a communicator to keep her there.

Work

Tell me about your first job, your other jobs, your best job, the advantages and disadvantages, your present job. How would you change things if you were the boss?

Sports

Which sports did you begin with, do you prefer, why? What are the advantages and disadvantages? Competitive vs. noncompetitive sports; money and sports; bloodsports. What value is there in sports for you? Tell me about your greatest success. If you could be a professional, which sport would you choose?

Music

What instruments do you play, would you like to play, do you like the most? Have you had lessons? Who are your favourite musicians? Why? How much do you listen to recordings, radio? What music makes you think of different moments in your life? What do you think of video clips? (See questionnaires.)

Travel

What countries have you visited? Tell me about your favourite places and trips, worst trip. Where would you like to visit if you had three months vacation now? Where would you go and what would you do, and who with?

Media habits

How much do you listen to the radio and watch television? Which programmes? What would make you change the station? Which newspapers do you read? What sections? What do you think of the media today?

Personalities

What kind of people do you like most, dislike most? What kind get on your nerves and what kind charm you? What are their qualities and why do you like them? Has your personality changed a lot?

Plans and goals

What are your plans and goals for the forthcoming year, five years? Where would you like to be in ten years and in what situation? Have the plans you've had in the past come true? If you could change something what would it be?

Literature

What authors and books do you like most (name your top five)? Why do you like them? Do you like books made into films, songs made into videos? What do you think of the literature you studied in school?

School

What do you remember most about your early schooling, good experiences and bad experiences? Did you like school when you first went (and then later)? What subjects did you like best and least? What teacher had the most impact upon you? Could you be a teacher? How would you be? What would you change about schooling?

Family

How many brothers and sisters do you have? Where are they and what are they doing now? What kind of parents do (did) you have? How were you raised? Do you like big families or small? Would you like to have many children? How does one bring up children?

Politics

Do you like or dislike politics? Why? Which party do you (or would you) belong to? Can you avoid politics? Which political questions interest you most? Are you more conservative or more liberal? If you were president . . .?

Sciences and technology

How has science and technology changed your life, the good and the bad? Could you live without a car, a telephone, a word processor, a television, electricity? How do you feel about robots, test tube babies, clones, medical experiments on animals, the automation of industry and the loss of jobs? What new things would you like to see science and technology do?

Weather

Are you affected greatly by changes in the weather? Do you prefer warm southern climates or cool northern ones? Do you think weather has something to do with the mentality of a nation?

Sleep and dreams

How much do you sleep at night? Do you take naps? Do you dream a lot? What about (if not too indiscreet)? Do you sleep walk? Where do you sleep best? When?

Other topics: movies, nature, history, psychology, zodiac signs, topics in the newspapers, etc. Such topics may be introduced by concrete referents such as articles, pictures, postcards, or realia.

19 CLL and the tape recorder

The approach and techniques of Community Language Learning (CLL) reflect somewhat the approaches of self-directed learning and of mirroring. Counselling Learning, CLL's predecessor, actually comes out of therapy. Its originator Charles A. Curran was a therapist who applied his ideas to education (see Stevick, 1980 for a good review). The name was changed to 'community' apparently because of the use of the techniques with groups which builds a sense of community, but also perhaps due to a certain mistrust among teachers who shy away from the idea that they are counsellors and therapists. I agree we should not pretend to be psychoanalysts in our work, but I also see that everyone now is a lay psychoanalyst and we all use psychological concepts when we think how best to teach and get along with each other. Mario Rinvolucri has said that psychology, more than applied linguistics, is the main feeder for ideas and methodology in language teaching in any case. Everyone is also a counsellor, implicitly or explicitly. We might also say that everything in life is therapy, for better or for worse.

In one community language learning technique students sit in a circle and say whatever they want to say in their native language. The teacher, who must be bilingual, goes behind each student who speaks and says the translation in her ear, which she repeats and records into a tape player once she feels she's got it. After a while the tape can be played and one hears only students saying things with meanings that they have created in a cohesive conversation with other students. This technique of course allows for self-direction in the content, but not necessarily in the **how**. However, such sessions typically end with a feedback session between the students and the teacher as to what they are doing and how they might do it differently. The technique of translating, in addition to serving language learning, allows teachers basically to mirror the linguistic meaning of the students and thus establish rapport.

In 1/1, especially with beginning students, the recording technique works very well. However, I don't translate at all. I record myself or the student saying things usually taken from my notes, or from something the student decides she wants on tape. If the student is secure enough, I do try to have her record her own voice as it will be more reinforcing when listening later. I've done it as a teacher and as a student with good success. The tape is concrete proof of my ability in a foreign language to get my meaning across as I listen to it. Upon subsequent listenings, the tape also has the power of positive reinforcement as the student hears no corrections from the teacher, only the communicative message said by the student. One actually has the feeling, both false and true, that one can communicate in the language. It's still a good idea for teachers to tape whole lessons for themselves in order to hear the way they use language and take turns. But for students, it is more focused and positively reinforcing if they only record their own voices.

Probably the most important aspect of CLL is the total acceptance of all of the messages by the teacher, without judgement. This promotes security in the students/clients and encourages self-exploration of what they really think, want, and can do. It implicitly forces them to take responsibility of the **what** in language learning.

McPherson (1987) presents an interesting case study in which she uses a counselling approach to discover strategies that a Japanese student is using and those he needs to learn. The problem sometimes occurs, as McPherson shows, when the student becomes so comfortable with the teacher that he has trouble communicating with others. 'The teacher's aim, therefore, is to form a bridge with the outside world, and to retain her objectivity regarding the student's communicative ability.' McPherson became more aware of confusing ways of communicating through listening to tapes of their conversations and by accompanying her student as he performed various tasks on the outside. By observing him, she was able to study the interactive procedures and better advise him about what was happening and what he needed in actual interaction. She concluded, 'this sort of approach may be particularly useful in dealing with students who have instrumental motivation, but experience an affective block when using the language in non-academic situations.'

John Morgan once showed me a counselling method of feedback that is similar to CLL and psychodrama. Basically, it consists of letting our clients speak about something for a few minutes and then giving the information back to them in a reformulated first person. For example, after one student tells me about her family I might say something like this:

'Thank you Silvia for telling me about your family. I'm going to tell you what I understood and then you can correct me or expand upon it afterwards. I heard you say, 'I have a big family. I am the middle child and it was nice to have older brothers and sisters to look after me and it was fun to help the younger ones . . .'

The exercise has many valuable qualities. In the above example (fabricated) the student may have said 'My old brother look at me and I pay attention my little sisters'. Reformulated, the corrections are made without a slap in the face and comprehensible input is given, a lot of it in fact. Misunderstandings can be clarified and additional information giving is encouraged. The student is listening to information that she already knows, but in language that the teacher adjusts to be more correct and perhaps a bit beyond the student's level – yet it is comprehensible. The fact that the information concerns the student personally makes for careful attentive listening for comprehension. The fact that the teacher uses 'I' encourages the student to take the language for her own, to identify with the teacher's role play. (Thanks to John Morgan for first demonstrating this to me.)

20 Video

Like any teaching material, video can be abused as the student takes a back seat. The principal idea is to keep the student interactively involved, and not to let the materials become the centre. This is done by getting the students to construct messages that are meaningful for them.

If 'a picture is worth a thousand words', then a video must be worth thousands more as it is made of thousands of individual frames. The trick in using video is not to use it as a T.V. or a film and just watch something straight through. The great thing about present-day video is that you can freeze the action where it is (Describe the image. What just happened?

What do you think will happen? What is your opinion so far about . . .?) and you can let the film turn with no sound (Describe in present progressive what is happening. What do you think they are saying?). Naturally this can be full of suspense, but carried too far it can also be frustrating. I've used video with adults and video clips with adolescents with great success. It is an extremely rich medium whose use will see further expansion.

Filming students with video can be very positive when they hear and see themselves performing adequately in English. For those training for sales presentations and speeches in English, taping them on day one and then again at the end can be excellent evidence of their progress as well as facilitating the teaching of communication skills.

21 The four skills
Reading, writing, listening, speaking

You may have students who want particular help in only one skill area: reading, writing, speaking, or listening. Of course we can focus on any one of these areas but it's difficult and unnatural to confine ourselves to any one. Crossover and reinforcement occur in any case. What we read, we may end up writing and saying; what we have overheard we may recognise in reading. When students understand this, they are usually more amenable to doing a variety of tasks, of course giving emphasis to the area of primary concern.

Reading

Reading is probably the most underrated language acquisition intensifier. The reason it is so underrated is that it seldom works when we force everybody to read the same texts, at the same speed. The opportunity that 1/1 teaching gives us is to find intensely interesting materials at the level of our students. Students only read a lot when it is pleasurable, i.e. not too difficult but nevertheless challenging at their intellectual level. In teaching 1/1 we get to know a student's level and interests much more than a teacher would in a general class. We then seem to find materials everywhere that are interesting to our students.

Short articles, short stories, and many graded readers are excellent stimulators. And just because students may have 'serious' jobs doesn't mean that they won't appreciate lively escapism or humour. I've had bankers enthralled by *Tom Sawyer* and engineers who liked reading Marilyn Monroe's biography in graded readers (Dainty 1986). But it should be their choice and seen as an offer from the teacher. I have turned myself into a kind of lending library which again takes my influence as a teacher beyond the mere class contact time. Providing them with the background or a summary of the story or article will usually give them enough curiosity to try. For younger students, comic books, hobby magazines (sports, fashion, music, etc.), and joke books (Snoopy, Denis the Menace, etc.) may get them hooked on books. Older students may enjoy these, too.

Writing

Some students may not like to write, nor need to. One student told me that she didn't like to write because in school she always got back more red than blue. Of course most students won't be interested in, and won't need to do essay writing as in school. A lot of fun can be had, however, with journals and diaries, letters, postcards, list-making, brainstorming, speech-writing, poetry, song-writing, and memos. When someone has a specific style and goal in writing, they should read materials which represent that style, for finally our writing is a reflection of what and how much we have read: like our passport, our writing tells people where we've been. The 1/1 lesson is, of course, ideal for tutoring writing (see Conference Centred Writing Chapter 7). Much composing, however, can be done outside the lesson, while reformulation and helping with redrafting can be done during the lesson. The student feels under pressure if composing while the teacher is waiting, and the teacher has feelings of uselessness. (For an excellent short account of the research on writing and some clear advice see Krashen, 1984.)

Listening

I had one student with eye problems for a while and he became hooked on books recorded on cassettes. There is an ever-increasing stock of such books read by well-known actors or the authors themselves. Not only are they providing students with literature, but also with listening comprehension practice. My student listened to several books that he had already read in French, thus he was not terribly frustrated when he couldn't catch little things because he already had a framework into which he could put the details he heard. Later he admitted to not knowing whether he remembered details from his reading in French or listening in English. Also, with 1/1 you can more easily guide your student in selective listening, and stop the cassette when the student needs time.

   In addition to books on cassettes, there are all sorts of radio shows, interviews, and songs that can be shared with a student. I loaned a copy of an interview with economist John Kenneth Galbraith to my banking students and they were enchanted. Once I even recorded a letter to my student with the sore eyes so he wouldn't have to read. Listening to other voices is of course a way to bridge the gap from what may be comfortably non-threatening conversation with the teacher to a less attentive and seemingly hostile world of strange accents and slurring.

Speaking

Speaking of course seems to be the main business of 1/1. Students want to speak a lot because they think they will improve a lot this way. It's true if they do speak a lot, confidence can grow and they may come to know how to express themselves better. But they may become too secure just speaking to the teacher in the same environment (as mentioned above). Changing the environment helps, but it is also good to arrange for other people to speak with them, such as language exchange partners (see Chapter 7), friends, family, etc. Another way to diversify speaking patterns is, of course, the use of role plays. 1/1 allows you the freedom to practise giving a real speech, selling products, responding to questions, etc. without the inhibition of other classmates.

The primacy of listening

Through my research and teaching, I have become aware of what could be called the primacy of listening in language learning. The normal development of language acquisition seems to be listening, speaking, reading, writing, although they are, in practice, seldom distinct from one another and they do contribute to each other's development. However, if adults are psychologically tied to the written word when learning a new language, their literacy may be a handicap when they wish to improve their spoken ability. Their literacy has somewhat replaced their uninhibited playful naturalness in language learning as children. They need to be reminded that language is first a spoken medium and only secondarily written. Students who read too much too soon, before having listened sufficiently to encode the sound system of the language, risk reinforcing their foreign accents through their own faulty subvocalisations of the language while reading (See Murphey, 1990b for more detailed discussion.)

22 The fifth skill
Living and thinking in a language

Getting a student to live and think in the target language may not be as difficult as it sounds. Basically, it means getting the students to form images of themselves as fluent speakers. When this is achieved, much learning goes on automatically and seems to defy description by researchers. Again, let me use the physical side of learning as an analogy.

Neurology research sometimes describes patients 'losing' part of their body image in their brain, while others who have had amputations often still feel their lost member. Oliver Sacks suggests that perhaps language could be seen in a similar light, i.e. of being *incorporate*, or not, as a new skill, a new member.

... the 'other side' of body-image losses are all the *incorporations* (into body image) of one's skis or one's scalpels – or for that matter, the car or the plane one pilots. Nothing feels 'natural', 'comes naturally' until it is incorporated.
... In learning sports (or, for that matter, ballet-dancing, or pancake-tossing) one *has*, I think, to start with a 'mimesis' – no abstract description or explication can be (to use our word again) incorporated as part of self. I suppose something of the sort is operative in language acquisition – when people are said to 'have an ear' ... and can (within minutes or hours) produce a sort of Swahili (or whatever) which *sounds* reasonable, and can communicate something, even though it is totally defective in vocabulary and grammar.   (personal communication)

Of course we recognise therein why children seemingly learn so much quicker than adults: they process information from imitation, and incorporate it, before adults can tell them it's difficult. Adults, trying to understand the complexity of a task, tend to look at it abstractly (but not necessarily holistically) and convince themselves it's difficult before giving themselves a chance simply to do it naturally. Perhaps that is why positive reinforcement and encouragement work as well as they do: we are somewhat forcing an image upon our student that she is not only somebody who can be a fluent speaker, but already is. The increase in confidence allows information to be processed in a 'childlikeness' posture in which 'I am what I see and hear'. (See Sacks, 1985, Gallwey, 1974, and Abraham, 1983.) Getting students to imagine scenes in which they perform admirably using the foreign language may help. Getting them to play the game of being a native speaker for extended periods will help more.
    A further way of 'living a language' is experiencing the immersion effect of involuntary rehearsal. Beginning and intermediate students in intensive learning situations sometimes experience what Barber (1980) has called a 'din in the head', the mental involuntary droning of language. Language seems to just flow through the mind uncontrolled, and often not understood, usually language that one has overheard in an immersion situation. Parr and Krashen (1986) have hypothesised that this may be a manifestation of Chomsky's LAD (Language Acquisition Device). Involuntary rehearsal shows that one has crossed a threshold of immersion such that information unconsciously being processed overflows into the conscious mind with the result that it may be even more deeply processed. It may also be that this 'din' can be voluntarily controlled and turned into inner speech (Vygotsky, 1934/1962).
    Hypothetically, this process can be induced to a certain extent through voluntary repetition of what one hears, through mental mimesis of all the qualities of what is heard. Songs seem to be one of the easiest sorts of texts with which to do this naturally, as songs often get stuck in our heads and repeat themselves involuntarily anyway. Asking students to have imaginary conversations with people in their heads, to sing songs to themselves, and to silently repeat (echoing) after people who speak as they would like to, may enable them to activate involuntary rehearsal.

23 Summary

This chapter has looked at a variety of materials, ideas and techniques:

- the student as primary material, commercial and authentic materials, concrete referents, how to adapt them and how to create them (a student's individual text book)
- the first classes and class planning
- techniques for using the student (C.V., questionnaires, agendas)
- techniques for monitoring what goes on (note-taking, listening, eye contact, mirroring)
- TPR language lessons in action
- advising and learner independence
- distance contact with the teacher (mail, telephone, journals, homework)
- start-up conversational topics
- the use of the tape player and video
- the four skills (reading, writing, listening and speaking)
- and the fifth skill 'being'.

In other words, Chapter 5 has dealt with some of the things that can actually be done in the 1/1 lesson, and beyond it, in our rapport with students. An integral part of teaching languages also has to do with guiding our students to be efficient learners. The next chapter will deal more with the practical aspects of setting up 1/1 teaching and staying in business.

6 Practical considerations

■■■ This chapter looks at the practical and organisational matters of 1/1 lessons and takes advantage of the information given in Chapters 2 and 3, as well as some 1/1 surveys, to provide a variety of alternatives.

The everyday concerns of organising and conducting private lessons are no great mystery. But everybody does things slightly differently. What follows are merely the ways some in the field have done things. Nothing is sacred, and experienced teachers will certainly find some sections naïve and others blasphemous. Stevick said it well with the title to his book, *Teaching languages: A way and ways* (1980). Basically, no one person's way is best for the rest of us, we all have to find our own individual ways, travel our own roads. Living and teaching well are processes of unique quality adjusting to our own individual environments. We may very well be doing many of the same things, using many of the same sign posts, but we are far from being the same (see Appendix 7 for a parable concerning eclecticism).

First the results of the few surveys concerning 1/1 teaching are given, then the major questions are addressed in separate sections.

1 Results from surveys of 1/1 teachers

Some general surveys ask the occasional question concerning 1/1 teaching with some surprising results. In a working conditions questionnaire in France, 53 per cent of the respondents said they taught 1/1 in addition to their regular teaching (Durban, 1988). In America, 77 per cent of 1,174 public school teachers (who were at a major conference and filled out questionnaires) use 1/1 configurations (pair and small group work) in their classrooms (see Chapter 7).

The only surveys that I know of exclusively concerning 1/1 teaching have been conducted in Switzerland. A resumé of the results is presented here without comment, since much of what is said has been already discussed in previous chapters or will be handled further on. Some views and stances are proposed different from those I have advocated, but it doesn't mean they are wrong or less valid, they are only different. Teachers should have as many options as possible for the ways to do things so that they can then choose those most fitting to their particular situation. When you know only one way to do things, or believe there's only one best way, you have no choice and are not capable of adapting to many different situations.

Teaching at home

In Switzerland, the Baden branch of the English Teachers Association Switzerland (ETAS) pioneered the first survey, that I know of, with thirteen members of their special interest group, 'Teaching at Home', ultimately filling out a questionnaire. The following profile emerges (from unpublished results compiled by Rossinelli and Frey, 1985):

None of the thirteen advertises for students; they find them through word of mouth, recommended by friends, neighbours, or other students. Most apparently accept all the students they have time for regardless of age, level, needs or personality, although a few consider personality more carefully before taking a student.

Half the teachers determine a student's ability through a written test and conversation, while a third do it by conversation alone (no mention of the other sixth). While most teachers teach only at home, negotiating cost and content, four teachers also teach in schools (one, two, or three people at a time) where the cost and content are set. Seven report giving lessons in their home, four in the student's home, and two in a rented room.

Lessons are given mornings, afternoons, and evenings, usually for between sixty and ninety minutes. While the frequency (e.g. once a week) of the courses is agreed upon, the duration (weeks, months, years) is seldom mentioned (by only one teacher). The biggest problems seem to be telephone interruptions and avoiding the family.

Students usually only pay for lessons they actually attend, although two teachers require payment for cancelled lessons (no-show, short-notice cancellation, or holidays).

While the average fee is between SFrs. 35 and SFrs. 40, this varies with several teachers as they adjust the cost according to how much specialised work is involved and the ability of the student to pay. None considers the cost of old-age pension, insurance, sick leave, and vacation when they set their fees. None of them asks for advanced payment and students either pay after each lesson or for a block of lessons.

They use a wide variety of materials, published and authentic, and the cassette recorder and blackboard, but very little video, computers, films, and slides.

Guidelines for teaching at home

The Baden 1/1 special interest group subsequently published guidelines for private home tutoring (Scarlin and Eliason 1986). They found the following points worthy of being established when giving private lessons:

- Purpose and length of lesson
- Venue
- Equipment
- Charge for lessons
- Method of payment
- Cancellation policy

While they allow for the negotiation of the duration of the course from time to time, they stressed that the student should be committed to the period agreed upon. Another thing they advised was that the lesson should finish on time regardless of the student's arrival time.

They advise that the venue should be 'ideally in a neutral place, but since most teaching is done at home in unbusinesslike surroundings, a quiet, undisturbed atmosphere is essential. See that your children "disappear", have no telephone interruptions (unplug or answer and hang up quickly) and if the doorbell rings answer it quickly as well. No coffee.'

While they have little to say concerning equipment, they have several suggestions concerning payment. They think it valid to charge more when travelling to the student and that a periodic increase in prices is normal. While they admit the method of payment varies, they see advanced payment having the advantage of encouraging your students to attend lessons. This also simplifies bookkeeping which they urge one to keep strictly.

They advised setting up a cancellation policy 'whereby both teacher and student are at liberty to cancel a lesson provided ample notice is given' or one might make it more explicit, saying the 'student forfeits the lesson if less than 24 hours notice is given' or the 'student pays a penalty fee (half the cost of a lesson or a fixed fee)'.

Second survey

The Baden branch conducted another survey asking for slightly different information and had eighteen responses.

Teachers reported teaching from one to ten students a week, for between one and fourteen hours (averaging about six hours a week). While 78 per cent gave lessons in their own home, 50 per cent gave lessons at their student's home and 33 per cent gave lessons in a school, office, or other (one teacher might give lessons in all three places). They taught all levels of English as well as some ESP (computer, business, and medical) and charged an average of SFrs. 39.60. However, the dispersion of rates went from SFrs. 18 to SFrs. 78. While none charged extra for travel costs, half charged for materials (books, cassettes, etc.) and six charged for cancellations.

The survey also asked what were the advantages and disadvantages for the teacher and the student in a 1/1 situation, with a few reporters contradicting each other. As you read them, try to decide which you agree or disagree with, and which you would qualify.

Student advantages
- facility in attending/scheduling lessons
- teacher's undivided attention
- tailor-made course and material for student's needs
- one-to-one contact promotes rapid learning. Teacher can correct on the spot, shift material, work according to student's progress

- personal contact – not restricted to 'intellectual' dimensions
- strong responsibility bond teacher–student
- no competition
- more input
- equal rights for teacher and student
- discussion, conversation opportunities
- no strict syllabus
- continuing where student left off at last lesson, no repeating for sake of the others
- possibility of cancelling

Teacher advantages

- time and opportunity to work on needs, experiment with methods, supplementary materials, not just course books
- flexibility of materials, freedom to try out various techniques and methods
- no waiting to try out something new, no frustration
- need adapt to only one pattern of learning personality at a time
- no conflicting preferences or needs
- seeing (hearing) rapid progress – rewarding/satisfaction
- teacher gets a lot of feedback
- can schedule lessons to suit self
- one to one
- may be well-paid for little preparation
- lessons more relaxed
- a challenge
- no paperwork, evaluation or syllabus
- tax-free earnings

Student disadvantages

- no other students to get ideas from, and to work and converse with
- no other students to compare self with
- pressure of performance – no slack time
- no chance to rest and digest
- class fixed on one person – hears only teacher's English
- doesn't feel among equals
- no group activities, can't practise third person singular
- teacher may advance too quickly
- very tiring
- difficult to get out of arrangement – can't just drop out
- can be expensive

Teacher disadvantages

- preparation of materials, meeting student's needs, maintaining enthusiasm
- very concentrated work for teacher, no interaction between students, consequently no 'breathing time' for teacher

- loss of overall view of language problems due to one to one situation
- time consuming preparation
- no possibility for games, rather dry
- boring, lacks stimulus of large class, less demanding
- last minute cancellation, irregularity
- if student is not responsive, teacher is probably too verbal
- teacher often does not charge full rate as she feels sorry for the poor student
- teacher has to adapt to one student's learning style and (possibly even) whims; may get boring or frightening if student is difficult and/or has trouble relating to other people. Teacher may feel obliged to please one person (servant role)

The respondents also said that they thought the demand for private lessons was large but that it takes time to build up a clientele by word of mouth. They gave their preparation time for a lesson as anything from a few minutes to several hours, depending on the client and subject. Asked what they enjoyed about private lessons, they gave a variety of responses:

- often more relaxed atmosphere, good conversations
- flexi-time for teacher and student
- freedom to try new sources
- giving undivided attention
- being own boss, getting to know students personally
- personal contact, interaction with intelligent students
- exchange of view which otherwise would not occur in classroom
- informal atmosphere – students are at ease

The same group later offered a list of eight conditions to give to students upon signing up for private lessons (December 1986 *ETAS Newsletter*). It is not clear if these conditions are part of a contract or simply a description as to how the teacher sees her rapport with the student.

Conditions for 1/1 teaching

1 Course books to be agreed upon by teacher and student. Books are not included in the price of the lesson. The price includes photocopying.
2 Lessons to start and end punctually.
3 Notice of cancellation . . . . hours in advance.
4 Payment for unexcused absences will not be refunded.
5 A reservation fee of . . . . may be required in the case of extended absence of longer than . . . .
6 Holidays to be agreed upon.
7 For termination of lessons, ... notice is required.
8 Prices subject to periodic review.

A one to one ETAS special interest group was later set up and a questionnaire distributed in the *ETAS Newsletter* (Winter 1987). But as yet no report of the results from it has come out. The activities of the various groups inside ETAS are evidence that you don't have to go it alone and that a lot can be learned from getting together and comparing notes. Setting up such groups in areas where many teachers are doing 1/1 is highly advisable for teacher development and professionalism.

2 Fees

Fees are subject to the supply and demand in your area. Of course one can create a demand with good publicity and by letting prospective students know there is an energetic teacher available who is flexible as to times and place of work. A bit of enquiry among other teachers doing similar work, or the salary in schools, will give you approximate figures.

Although everybody is interested in knowing what everyone else earns, cultural taboo often prevents us from asking and some teachers are shocked or evasive if we do. I've found it better to ask not what 'you' earn but what 'a teacher' earns in such and such a situation in the area.

In Switzerland the normal rate seems to be from SFrs. 40 to SFrs. 60 (see Appendix 6 for exchange rates at time of printing) in big cities, more if you are attached to a school or language consultancy service, whereas in quaint Neuchâtel SFrs. 30 seems fair, especially since at some private language schools teachers receive under SFrs. 30 for an hour class teaching ten to twenty students. After a while, with more experience and an established clientele, a periodic increase in fees is normal procedure. Some teachers' and schools offer discounts with the scheduling of a certain number of lessons.

As a student, I gave lessons in exchange for laundry services and meals with my neighbours. As I began with the business community, I charged SFrs. 30 an hour. Starting my second year and having a position at the university, I didn't need as many students and I upped my rates to SFrs. 40 an hour. Often with the business contact, meals were also included, thus making it actually a SFrs. 50 to SFrs. 80 an hour lesson. Several 1/1 teachers have told me that charging higher fees brought in more clients. Apparently some prospective students reason that low fees mean an unprofessional teacher and that higher fees indicate a more dynamic teacher. This attitude, of course, is probably subject to change in different cultures. For comparison purposes, in Japan, one of the most lucrative EFL markets, private teachers at present are getting around SFrs. 50 an hour (Redfield, 1986).

3 Collecting fees and cancellations

Some students prefer to pay on the spot, others to be billed. Business men and women often want receipts because their company reimburses them for lessons (also for the meals). Buying a little receipt book looks more professional than writing things out on paper and it's an easy way for you to keep records if you work a lot with business people.

Teachers sometimes insist on prepayment, fixed times, and dates, thus they are paid whether the student shows or not. This is certainly one way to do it and I imagine some students prefer the fixed regularity of the lessons. However, I feel that many executives also appreciate the flexibility that a private teacher is able to provide and that a school cannot.

Some teachers argue that without prepayment students feel less motivated to come to lessons and then the teacher has prepared something and wasted her time. I would argue that prepayment might make it too much of an obligation. Dates and times that are set (further than the next one) may be too constraining for busy executives. The flexibility, without pecuniary loss for cancellations, puts the student more in an equal encounter situation. Finally, as a teacher I prefer not to have the student come if she doesn't feel like it or if she is too busy. With proper forewarning, I accept cancellations. And my students will in turn accept it from me if something comes up.

I have occasionally had cancellations that only arrived a few hours before the meeting. I say 'no problem', and I think they appreciate it and are quick to make another appointment. The only time when a student didn't show up, I was paid anyway, which I feel is an honest thing to do.

In countries or environments where teachers run a great risk of being stood up and not paid, I would of course recommend prepayment. This doesn't mean that you cannot be somewhat flexible as well. But you should make it clear from the beginning with your clients that they must contact you at least 24 hours ahead of time (or some such deadline) in order to change a class and not lose the money for a lesson. Where no-shows are not a problem, I think postpayment with flexibility built into your professional style will encourage a lot of business and help create equal encounter situations.

For severe problems there are sometimes legal rights offices for small business people where you can go to get free advice. Also, both TESOL France and ETAS (English Teachers Association Switzerland), and probably other language teachers' associations, have 'working conditions' subcommittees which try to let teachers know their rights (see also Dingwall, 1988). Needless to say that there is usually little help for those who don't have work permits or valid residency.

4 Length of lessons

I charge by the hour. But I don't look at the clock and if it lasts an hour and a quarter I don't mind, especially if the student is buying lunch. I do charge another SFrs. 20 per half hour. With some students an hour may seem like a long time, and with others two hours will fly by unnoticed. I wouldn't be averse to meeting for quick thirty minute conversation breaks or having five to ten minutes with a student on the telephone. Flexibility concerning the length of a lesson, like the place and appointment time, is very attractive to many business people. Others, however, may prefer the regularity of same time, same place, same length each week.

How often one meets during a week or month is again to be negotiated with the client. I find that once or twice a week leaves enough time for things to happen and a rich amount of conversational topics to accumulate. Executives with their busy schedules will often only want once a week, unless they are going abroad soon, in which case once a day may be preferable.

Intensive, multiple-hours in a few days or weeks, are also usually accompanied by a reduction in the hourly fee.

5 Meeting places

In Chapter 3 we discussed the advantages and disadvantages of six places where a lesson might be held: in a school, at the teacher's home, at the student's home, the student's business, in a café/restaurant, or while doing some activity. Usually the teacher already has a place in mind where she will give her lessons. However, allowing the students to choose the place puts more control in their hands. We also noted that changing meeting places periodically may add variety and inspire other language and conversational strategies.

As we saw with CIWA, the 1/1 service company, the possibility of teaching the student at the student's home or place of work may be a big selling point. However, the great number of teachers who give lessons in their homes quite positively proves the viability of this arrangement as well.

6 Getting clients

My first endeavours to advertise were poor. But I think I've learned a few things since:

1 Personal contact seems to be the best seller.
2 Your best advertising will always be your satisfied clients.

Getting the first few clients may be the most difficult. Letting your friends and students know you are looking for students and are a serious teacher will bring you more by word of mouth.

If you have contacts in businesses who can introduce you to possible clients and you can manage an unpaid first prospective meeting, I feel you have the proverbial foot in the door. Going to banks and businesses without having a name is not usually advisable. Announcements put up on bulletin boards and in newspapers may bring in the odd student (the odd ones are often the best) but it doesn't seem to be the best source.

One thing I would advise, for someone going into it seriously, would be a business card to hand out to prospective clients, or to leave at businesses. Something like:

Another technique that a few teachers have admitted to using is that of calling businesses in which employees should speak English, and speaking to the personnel in English on the telephone to see if they can speak well enough. One teacher even records the conversations and then plays the tapes when she goes to ask for a job as proof that she is needed. She offers intensive telephone receptionist English and re-records her students again after a week's course of exercises to show the employers that her teaching works.

7 Travel and photocopying expenses

Generally speaking if the travelling is only five to fifteen minutes across town, it should already be included in the cost. This of course is something to be determined at the outset. It is quite unprofessional to decide after lessons have started that students should pay you more for the distance.

It is usually clear that books and cassettes are paid for by the student, however, a reasonable number of photocopies should also be part of the original fee. If, however, I photocopy a twenty page article for someone, I will usually ask for the few francs it cost. Again, hard and fast rules in these areas reduce our ability to adjust to each new situation as it presents itself. Setting up general guidelines a priori is OK, but don't let them tie you down.

8 Training in 1/1 and teacher development

Wilber (in 1986) and Smit (in 1987) gave presentations at IATEFL annual conferences. During 1987/88 Murray and Neithammer gave a series of workshops throughout Switzerland on teaching 1/1. No university course which deals with the topic exists to my knowledge. International House Hastings offered a five day TEFL Workshop on 1/1 teaching in April 1987. The ideas of each of these have been dealt with to some extent in Chapter 3.

Otherwise, for development, teachers are best advised to meet others in their areas who are teaching 1/1, form discussion groups and possibly publish case studies (see next section). Usually other teachers feel flattered to be asked about how they go about teaching 1/1 and welcome the opportunity to share experiences.

Of course the plethora of workshops and materials for classroom teachers will in most cases feed the 1/1 teacher who knows how to adapt and adjust them.

9 Publication of 1/1 case studies

The teaching situations are very different in different countries, and even in one city clients of many kinds will exist. Admittedly, even this book is culture bound by the experiences the author has had in his particular environment. I would expect the conditions, problems, and solutions to be at least slightly different in different countries. The way we teach in Japan, Kuwait, Venezuela, and Italy will each have its own character. For those teaching in Japan, a valuable source is *A Guide to Teaching English in Japan* compiled by Charles Wordell (published by *The Japan Times*, 1985). There is one chapter by William McBean on 'Private Lesson Teaching'.

If teachers are fortunate enough to meet other 1/1 teachers, special interest groups can spring up and they can share experiences while they help each other to adapt. One way for teachers to help each other out and enrich their own teaching is to compile 1/1 case histories. This can be organised along the following lines.

One to One Case Studies Publication
In order to share 1/1 experiences, we are asking members of our group to write up one of their interesting case studies. Maximum length is three to four pages, but even one interesting page would be fine. Each case history should answer some or all of the following questions (if they are relevant) and perhaps others that are not mentioned:
1 Briefly what is the teacher's situation: Do you give a lot of 1/1 lessons, live from it, just do it occasionally, since when?
2 Who is the client? Age, profession, background, characteristics, how was contact made?
3 When were lessons, for how long, over how many months, etc.? e.g. twice a week for an hour for three months.
4 Where did you meet? Office, school, home, café, etc.
5 What was the content? Business English, test, conversation enrichment, grammar, vocabulary?
6 How did you teach? What techniques did you use? Through conversation, tapes, writing, etc.

7	Explain in a narrative fashion how the lessons progressed or changed.
8	What was the affective (emotional) atmosphere?
9	What progress was made, in what areas?
10	Things that you learned from the experience, or observations you would like to share.
11	Questions that are left unanswered and which you would like to see addressed by others. Things to think about.

Teachers of course should not use the client's real name and can themselves write their contribution anonymously. If you wish you could write two, with the stipulation that one be a very positive experience and the other somewhat negative. (We potentially learn more when things go wrong than when they go right, although they may be the most difficult to write about and relive.)

Teachers are encouraged to work 1/1 with another teacher on their drafts before submitting them to make sure they are clear and readable. Exchanging your work for criticism before giving them to the editor tunes them in much more to 'reader needs' and saves the editor a lot of frustration.

Even if only five people write up case histories, they provide a wealth of information at least for each other. If others outside the group desire copies they could be sold to recoup the cost of photocopies and compilation. Funds could also be requested from teachers' associations for the photocopying or printing costs.

Teachers' groups are well known for being heavily administered by a few with little input from other members who just come to take notes. In this way, more will be encouraged to get into the act.

Finally, the group could ask a pair of teacher trainers, or a few of their own members, to write an introduction and/or conclusion to the collection, as well as do some editing, trying to draw parallels between the different cases and main themes. If the collection proves useful and popular, other sets of case histories could be collected. Teachers could also do their own survey and publish the results along with the collection of case studies.

I foresee more and more case histories coming out, not just for 1/1 but for classroom teaching as well, simply because they are easier to read than many theoretical texts. Some methodology books may be somewhat preachy and abstract with their 'do's and don'ts'. Case studies don't tell you how to do it, but describe how it was done in different environments. (See Peck, 1988, for the rationale behind case studies and some good examples in classroom teaching).

7 Implications for regular classroom teaching

After teaching 1/1 for some time, I said to myself, 'Hey Murphey, if you really think the characteristics of 1/1 make language learning so efficient, what elements of it could you incorporate into your regular classroom/group teaching?' This chapter contains much more than the answer I gave myself at the time because I have had a few years to experiment, read, and to think things over; not to mention write a few drafts of this book.

1 Restructuring discourse in the classroom

Sinclair and Brazil (1982), in their analysis *Teacher Talk*, reveal the 'pseudo-dialogal situation' found in many classrooms. They see the problem and the solution as follows:

... the teacher dominates the talk in quantity, range and degree of control.
... If it is desired to enhance the opportunities for the pupils, a fundamental restructuring of the discourse is required.

This restructuring of discourse is especially important in a learning environment like a school, for as Sperber and Wilson show, 'Speakers who are not aware of their hearer's disposition in the matter risk asking them for too much effort or providing them with too few effects.' (1986:132) That is to say that teachers who don't know much about the socio-psychological set of their students may be asking for too much effort with too few rewards, creating frustration and promoting abandonment.

If I walk into a class and immediately start lecturing on the present perfect, the students will most likely construct invisible walls to protect themselves from the onslaught. If I want to interact with the students and make sure they are implicated in the lesson I will have to do some restructuring. With adolescents I might begin 'Has anyone seen Michael Jackson's latest video?' Then I would get them to write five questions they would like to ask anybody in the room (using the present perfect). Next, I would have them actually ask each other the questions. It would be noisy for a while, but that's OK.

Then they would have to choose a partner and tell them all the answers they got. Then maybe each student would choose one question and answer to tell the whole class about. Hopefully in this way I have shifted the structure of discourse somewhat towards 1/1 conversational structure, and made it relevant to them by showing they can ask about anything (we might give more examples before beginning), and I have given them a certain amount of responsibility to create the content and choose who they want to interact with.

Sinclair and Brazil further suggest the use of theatre work to change the *ex cathedra*, teacher-fronted discourse in order to allow and encourage more natural interaction:

[In drama] by exercising the imagination, pupils can simulate characters and situations that allow a wider range of speaking rights than the classroom normally offers them. The teacher adopts a role something like that of a producer at rehearsal.... Its value does not lie so much in the controlled practice of discourse as in its motivating power and release from the constraints of the usual discourse in the classroom. [Small groups and pairs] develop sub-conversations where the pupils have to take all the initiatives. ... Almost any subject matter can provide the focus of the talk. (1982:7)

2 Equalising encounters

The most obvious implication from previous chapters for the classroom would be to equalise to some extent our encounters with students. The school environment implies authority, and with the giving of grades and marks, teachers cannot deny the power that they hold. The reality of the situation is such that the teacher will always be at some distance from an equal encounter. (In fact, perfectly equal encounters are an ideal. But it is knowing that the other person has knowledge and abilities that we don't possess that allows us to accept being the weaker partner, at times, with humility, and not to take advantage of our position when we are the stronger.)

Nevertheless, much can be done to reduce the distance between the teacher and students through allowing them to take control of much of what goes on in classes (Dickinson, 1987) and by using them and their interests as the subject matter of the instruction (Rivers, 1976). The next few sections describe how this might be done in more detail.

3 Students as teachers

One of the best ways to instil responsibility and a positive image of the class is to get students to take an active part in the running of a course. Bassano and Christison (1988) list several areas in which students can take a more active role, starting simply with the classroom environment in which students can do such things as arranging the chairs, handing out materials, keeping attendance, making announcements, collecting money for coffee or an extracurricular activity.

Students can be more actively involved in the actual teaching through **peer tutoring**. When they have the responsibility for teaching each other, motivation increases and the intensity of interaction is augmented. Amazingly enough, the tutor usually makes even more progress in the process. As was remarked with our case histories, teaching others is one of the best ways to learn.

One way to do this is for the teacher to teach one student in a quality 1/1 optimal teaching situation and then this student teaches another until the second student has learned it sufficiently. Then both of these students can teach others. Going back to my story of the skiers (page 4), these students can also take turns in being the first in line.

Students can also do a lot of the correcting in the classroom. Bassano and Christison (1988) feel **peer correction** not only saves the teacher a lot of work but is excellent pedagogy:

The moment students finish a written task and hand it in, their motivation is at its highest because they are interested in finding out if their answers are correct. Most teachers collect work, take it home to correct, and return it the following day. By then, the students may have lost interest. They may glance over their work briefly (perhaps counting the red pen markings) and then throw the work away. An important moment for the student has been lost, and several hours of teacher time have been wasted.

The authors suggest having students work in pairs, after doing an assignment, to try to spot anything that needs changing in each other's work. Then they can write any questions that they have on the board and the teacher deals with them one at a time. Students learn that 'this kind of immediate feedback is more helpful and instructive than red pen markings'.

Bessano and Christison also feel that students can be made to participate more with each other and in the class by setting their own goals, by selecting material to be studied, and finally by giving feedback as to what they learned, what they found difficult to learn, and what was enjoyable or tedious.

4 Pair and small group work

Pair work is simply 1/1 pairs in the classroom. It allows students to practise the full range of integrated skills that make up communication in a foreign language, and to practise it with one person at a time, not in front of a whole group. School can be a place where the student can dare to risk communication, more than out on the street, but we have to organise the classroom activities to be as non-threatening as possible. The advantage of this sheltered environment for communicating is lost if students are only allowed to speak one at a time with the whole class as audience. It is frightening enough to do this in your native language, let alone a foreign language.

A number of researchers have shown with a variety of tasks that the performance of children in pairs or groups is usually superior to that of children working alone, and that later this superiority carries over into individual performance (Doise et al. 1981, Perret-Clermont and Mugny 1985).

It seems that '. . . individuals need to coordinate their different and sometimes conflicting points of view and this leads them into a restructuring of their views and understanding. Cognitive conflicts created by social interaction appear then as the locus at which the power driving intellectual development is generated.' (Light and Perret-Clermont 1986)

Apparently Piaget, as a theoretician, had recognised the importance of social interaction for cognitive development, but neither he nor his close followers paid much attention to it. However, of late, psychologists have begun researching more and more child–child interaction, peer facilitation, the role of contradiction, and the possibility in these to 'decentre' the child's thought, and stimulate cognitive development.

Strong (1983), however, states that simply throwing children together to interact is not enough; in such a situation only the naturally verbose and extroverted will make much progress. Instead he suggests that teachers must create situations in which students want and need to interact in order to perform a task or to reach a common goal. This corresponds with Light and Perret-Clermont's idea above that social interaction that results in cognitive conflict (i.e. differing views and interpretations) promotes intellectual development.

In Pica's (et al. 1987) and Long's (1983, 1985) terms, interaction is normal, but interaction modification (comprehension checks and clarification requests) may be the necessary ingredient to spark language acquisition. The simple fact is that not much modification of interaction happens in teacher-fronted classes. It happens much more when only two people are talking to each other, and more when they are on relatively equal ground. Thus, when there is cognitive conflict (non-understanding) in a teacher-fronted class, it seems, it is simply accepted without the interactive effort given to resolve it, or it is ignored, whereas in 1/1 the parties feel freer to attempt to modify interaction and to resolve conflict.

August (1987) organised an experiment in peer tutoring which makes the above even more concrete. She had limited English speaking children (LES) teach fluent English speaking (FES) children a game or activity that only the LES children had learned earlier in the day. Thus, the weaker partner (linguistically) in the interaction had information that the stronger didn't have. The FES children were motivated to understand the information and the LES children to share their knowledge. Not only was there an equalling of the encounter, which had noticeably positive results in after class play activities, but a situation was organised in which 'cognitive conflict' (understanding the information for the FES child and communicating the information through a foreign language for the LES child) could be resolved through interaction. The gains in English language learning were significant for the LES children.

Pica *et al.* (1987) concluded that without spoken interaction, premodified input (graded syllabuses and simplified texts and tapes) was of limited use.

Instead, results 'suggest that if oral interaction between students and teacher is encouraged, even *ungraded* syllabuses and materials may provide input that will become comprehensible. Perhaps the most significant pedagogical implication to be drawn is that any teacher or method that facilitates a realignment of the traditional roles of teacher and student, so that students can take greater initiative or assume more responsibility for their own learning, is likely to encourage in-class oral interaction, which in turn can increase comprehension of input.' (pp. 754–5)

As was noted above, instead of having students work only with the teacher, teachers can immensely improve the quality of student output, and save teacher-time, by going through steps in which students must interact with each other. Indeed, it would seem that this is becoming a more and more popular configuration with teachers in general. At two major conventions of school teachers in the U.S. in 1988, 1,174 veteran teachers reported on the types of teaching they found most effective:

Types of Teaching

Fewer students makes for more effective teaching, say veterans at all grade levels. Teachers were asked to rank five common types of instructional activity in order of their effectiveness. Here are percentages who ranked each type in their top two:

	Percentages of teachers			
	Elem. school	Middle/ Jr. high	High school	All teachers
Work in small groups	84.4	81.7	70.9	78.2
Working one-on-one	78.6	77.1	75.8	77.4
Classwide activity	27.7	29.4	34.6	30.8
Lecture to class	7.6	9.5	17.5	11.5
Seat work	4.1	6.1	6.3	5.2

(reported in USA TODAY, August 31, 1988)

It should be noted that these are figures of teachers who have given some of their time to professional development during the summer months. They may not represent the majority of the profession and not necessarily your average teacher. Teachers who care enough about doing a good job to give up some vacation time also read journals and experiment in their classes. A survey of all teachers would probably yield different statistics, hopefully not much different. But for our purpose here, it is encouraging to see that the professionally active teachers overwhelmingly are convinced of the effectiveness of 'one-on-one' and small groups in their classes.

To illustrate how this might be done, what follows is an example in what is normally a very 'student-alone-against-the-world' composition class:

Task for the class: Write a composition on the value of music
Teacher's instructions:
1 This is a huge topic. In pairs brainstorm as many questions, ideas, and aspects concerning the general topic, this may make it more specific or larger. You have 3 minutes.
2 Compare your brainstorming list with another group. 2 minutes
3 Now choose a topic that you think you would like to write about, outline briefly what you think you might say about it, and tell your partner about it. 5 minutes
4 Write (with soft music in the background): 20 minutes. Pause when you like and let your partner read what you've written – give comments and suggestions to your partner and try to tell your partner what you've understood from the reading and where you think he or she is going with the composition.
5 Write (and rewrite) 15 minutes. Now give your partner your composition. Partner check (any variety of composition skills that the teacher may have gone over the past few classes, or things to be emphasised at this time). Partners make further comments and suggestions.
6 Homework. Students rewrite composition considering the comments made by their partners, give it to their partners for proof reading and feedback one more time. If necessary rewrite it again. Turn it in in three days with partner's name and yours.

There's a lot of interaction above in what is normally a non-interactive class. The teacher is now free to circulate and give valuable 1/1 advice where needed most and to leave students alone so they can get on with learning from each other, making their writing more than just teacher-reader based but peer-reader based (see CCW section 8 this chapter).

Another example might make this interaction principle even more concrete for you. In a school setting, I wanted to give a test of the different vocabulary and structures that we had covered the last few weeks. I asked the students in pairs to brainstorm all the things that they thought they had learned and that should be on a test. Then they had to go into groups of fours and exchange their papers and discuss whether they agreed with what the other partners suggested be on the test. Some were crossed off, some were added on, and there was a lot of negotiation going on. I collected the lists, condensed them into one list, and in the next lesson distributed copies to each person, instructing them to formulate the actual test questions. They each did so, and then in pairs verified that there were no mistakes in the questions. I told them that the next day a certain number of the questions they wrote would be on the test. In the remaining quarter of an hour they were permitted to read every other student's test and to go and ask the author the answer if they didn't know it. Needless to say it was an intense fifteen minutes. What is more, I found that they said they had learned things that I was unaware of. As Allwright has illustrated in several articles (1984a&b, 1986a&b), teachers and students don't always agree on what goes on in the classroom, what is taught and what is learned. The above exercise allows teachers to adjust their perceptions to those of their students.

Byrne (1987:33) provides a list of the problems that teachers usually voice concerning pair work. The following is a summary of these complaints and how he sees their resolutions:

1 **too much noise** – First of all it's a good sign. If it disturbs the neighbouring classes, about all you can do is explain to the students and ask them to do it quieter, or in a whisper.
2 **students make mistakes** – Good preparation and notes on the board will prevent most mistakes. If a lot of mistakes are being made, the teacher can stop and explain it one more time. Finally though, most pair work is done for developing fluency and the great amount of practice far outweighs a few mistakes.
3 **students won't work properly** (they might just speak in their mother tongue or do nothing at all) – If you know which students do this a lot, you can attend more to them. But just because some students misbehave is not a good reason to deprive the others of the practice. 'When you are teaching the whole class, you can't be sure that the students are co-operating just because they are keeping quiet.' (p. 34)
4 **students expect the teacher to teach** – The teacher should be prepared to justify pair work and explain why it is worthwhile, especially in countries where lecture style teaching is the norm and students are not accustomed to such procedures.

Cooperative small groups

Bejarano's (1987) research in Israel found that cooperative small groups were superior to teacher-fronted classes. Bejarano's two approaches for cooperative learning were Discussion Groups (DG) and Student Teams and Achievement Divisions (STAD).

For DGs, classes are divided into smaller groups which treat different topics or problem-solving issues. Each person, or pair, in the group is assigned subtasks that they must perform before the information is given back to the group for synthesis and finally presentation to the class. For example, pollution might be the main topic for all groups. Different groups may be in charge of air, water, land, and sound pollution. Inside each group, pairs might be divided up into those who look for information in books, in magazines, through interviews, and realia. The three things each pair might concentrate on are how it was in the past, the conditions now, and future predictions. The whole group would be responsible for discussing the information they had gathered and for making the synthesis. A few leaders would make sure that everyone had a part in the presentation and that it was entertaining and informative. (N.B. this is my imagined example, not Bejarano's.)

For STADs, students are ranked by the teacher in the order of their ability and teams are made even by mixing the strong with the weak. The teacher presents a teaching unit and then pairs of students are given worksheets to work through and study, the strong helping the weaker, and all of them training together. At the end they are given individual tests and the average for the group is compared with that of the other groups. Thus, since it is in the interest of the group that each student does well, they help each other learn. (Bejarano's fine article is highly recommended for further clarification of these two models.)

In the same experiments, observations in the classes 'indicated that all students were involved in interaction and communication among themselves during at least 40 per cent (and sometimes up to 80 per cent) of class time, whereas in the traditional classes the teacher lectured during at least 80 per cent of class time' (p. 495). The authors concluded that the small groups were more efficient because they presented an immediate need for every individual in the group to participate. This corresponds with Hatch's finding that 'linguistic forms are acquired and used productively only when it assumes a critical role in transmitting essential information' (1978:472). In other words, language must be meaningful for the students involved in order for them to use, process, and acquire it. They have to have a reason for use other than the vague 'to learn the language'.

Understandably, students who were in the small groups achieved high marks in tests of listening comprehension, much higher than the control group taught as a whole class group. This was due to their increase in instrumental listening and their obligation to react in a set time. Bejarano says the two cooperative small group configurations complement each other and both could be used with the same class. In related studies, Krashen (1981) found students prefer listening to friends than to teachers and Cohen (1984) reported that during a whole-class lesson only 25 to 50 per cent of the students actually listen to the teacher.

5 Self-instruction/learner independence

In addition to letting students become more responsible for the planning and running of group courses, as Bassano and Christison (1988) have suggested above, they also have special information stocks which we can tap, whether this be about their own country, about their professions and hobbies, or simply the individual way each of our students perceives the world.

Some years ago, I was kindly allowed to sit in on some in-company English classes in a large international firm in London. The class was composed of executives from France and was conducted as a kind of board meeting. Each student had the responsibility to research and describe the usefulness of some grammatical point, exercise, vocabulary, etc. They became the teachers and presented their findings to the class, as one would do at board meetings. This cut down on the unequal encounter situation and had them playing a familiar role while making executive decisions. The teacher when more actively involved used Silent Way elicitation and modification techniques which were devoid of any harsh correction. These executives from Paris appreciated the opportunity to take charge for a portion of their learning.

As Dickinson (1987) explains, semi-autonomy and responsibility can already begin in the school. The early steps are simply in giving students choices, e.g. topics for discussion or a composition, different library books, where to sit, or who to have as a partner. Later it means getting students to generate their own choices, and finally their own means. It's rather a continuum between being totally directed through gradually more and more self-selection of what and how they learn in order to become ever more efficient learners. Finally, we can often collaborate with students on the actual programme of the course: 'There is great scope for engaging students in the negotiating language of their education' (Sinclair and Brazil 1982:8).

An example

The last sixteen summers I have had the good fortune to teach in a language and sports camp in which there are few administrative prerequisites and thus I have been free to choose the materials and methods for teaching groups of international children from seven to seventeen in three week programmes. As much as possible, these last few years, I have tried to pass on this freedom to my students in varying degrees. There are three general age groups and different things that I can do to let them have as much control over what we do as possible.

With the seven to ten and the eleven to thirteen year olds, beginners through advanced, we sing a variety of songs and jazz chants and play a variety of language learning games the first few days from which they can later choose for further activities. They sit where they want to, next to whom they wish and we often simply end up on the floor. The more advanced (in all age groups) write a journal the first five minutes of every class and can write anything they wish, or they can write 'I don't want to write today', but they must explain to me why (in writing). I might say to them, today I want you to describe someone in your journal (they choose who), to write about something in the past tense (they choose when). If there are several pages in their books of equal difficulty, I can let them choose which ones to do, and we don't all have to be doing the same thing.

With the fourteen to seventeen year olds I have become more direct. I tell them they have English class one hour a day and that is the only given. We can do anything we wish to do as long as it is contributing maximally (in my judgement) to improving their English. I let them know that in my judgement the choice being theirs will contribute greatly to their motivation and language learning. I have them discuss in pairs what they did in past classes that they enjoyed and what they think would be fun and profitable to do now. In addition to them discussing this in pairs and then with the group they fill out questionnaires concerning their preferred activities. Of course there are usually diverse desires, some want grammar and some video clips, and thus there usually ends up being a mixture of things to do that is accepted by everyone because everyone had a say in organising the course. Occasionally they will surprise me with a particularly challenging idea like writing and making our own video, which we actually did.

We continue to discuss and renegotiate as the course progresses. Usually half way through a session, I have them write in their journal about what we have done so far, saying what activities they think they learned from and which ones were enjoyable, as well as which ones weren't. At the end of the course, on the final test (basically created by them) the last page asks for feedback concerning the English class and the camp in general, positive and negative. They are told that the last page, without their name, will be given to the camp director and that their comments may have some impact on how to improve the camp. Thus, they fill it in responsibly and with many interesting comments for the administration.

Finally, I believe most young people are responsible only when they are given the freedom to develop responsibility. Practice in making their own pedagogical decisions is necessary if we ultimately want them to become efficient learners, independent of merely required learning. **When students realise that finally they are in control of what and how they learn, they become many times over more powerful in teaching themselves than the schools with which they begin**. Then when they do choose to study in a school, with a 1/1 teacher, with a computer or library, or simply by themselves, it is because they have found it to be the best configuration for them to learn in at the time, not simply because there is only one choice available.

Still, a warning should be given to teachers that many students probably don't want, and are not able, to take a lot of the responsibility for their learning, at least in the beginning. A teacher may have to provide a lot of direction at first, while slowly introducing self-direction methods. Again, each student is different, some may never want the responsibility. It would be a mistake to go into a teaching situation assuming the students want and are able to make all the decisions. One should be prepared to lead as much as necessary, but it is worth periodically seeing if they can take on more and more responsibility.

6 Programme variations using 1/1 principles

Below are a few more concrete ideas for language programmes and classroom organisation to encourage 1/1 encounter principles.

Language Exchange Programme (Universities of Florida & Neuchâtel)

A lot of people want to learn languages. If we could find all the French speakers wanting to learn English and match them up with the English speakers wanting to learn French, they could help each other out. But ideally we would want them to be involved in some sort of natural activity and to converse about things they mutually like. Also, if half the time they were speaking French and half the time they were speaking English, they would be reversing strong and weak partner roles. That would hopefully give them humility when in the strong role and courage when in the weak role, for they would spend half the time in each.

My first experience with this idea on a large scale was the project developed at the University of Florida by Mike Pyle in the late 1970s. It consists simply of finding two different language groups wishing to practise each other's language. In Florida, it was mainly our Spanish speaking ESL students and the Anglo-natives wishing to improve their Spanish. These last were not necessarily students, but researchers, business people, etc., who wanted practice because of periodic dealings with Spanish speakers.

The only work for the administrators of such a programme is formulating a questionnaire for interested participants to fill out (see appendix 5) and the pairing up of suitable partners based principally upon shared interests. All of this happens during the first few weeks of a term although it could be a permanent set-up. Keeping all of the participants' phone numbers and addresses allows you to check up at the end of the year how successful it was, either by phoning around or sending a questionnaire.

In Florida, with more than 35,000 university students, candidates were plentiful and administrating the programme became a year-round affair. In Neuchâtel, I managed such a programme for about forty native English speakers with the same number of university English Seminar students. However, with such a small population I administered it for only a month each fall, putting up publicity, handing out forms, and pairing people up.

Unfortunately, some partners will be mismatched personality-wise or schedule-wise and will simply stop (after the administrator sends each participant his partner's form, scheduling and contacting is left up to them). However, they are encouraged to try again with another partner if the first one doesn't work out.

I believe that if even a small percentage is helped to make contact and have realistic exchanges, it is worth the few administrative hours. End of the year questionnaires by telephone revealed consistently that 40 per cent had continued through each year. I also feel it's part of my job as a teacher to encourage my students to take the risk of stepping into real communication situations.

Conversation groups

Another programme variety is to organise small conversation groups, three to five people usually, as done by Lund (1981) at the University of Florida English Language Institute (ELI).

Basically what Lund did was recruit vivacious, but sensitive, university students to act as conversation group leaders with ELI students. The group leaders were hired through the system called 'work study'; the U.S. government paid most of the wages of university students who qualified for special funding (who were then termed 'work-study students'). This 'work-study' system meant that the ELI could hire U.S. undergraduates at very little cost to the programme (while the students earned minimum wages) and had the advantage over using volunteers because, as the old saying goes, 'you can't fire a volunteer'. That is, Lund could make demands on the U.S. undergraduates in terms of productivity and training.

The ELI administrators had recognised the need for the students to practise spontaneous spoken English with the natives. Although the students were living in an anglophone community, they were still hesitant to have contact with natives. Their classroom English was good but they needed some way to cross the bridge from structured classroom learning to spontaneous use in everyday conversation.

The students at the ELI had the option to participate by simply filling out a short form at the beginning of the term. They were put into multilingual groups as much as possible, to avoid the temptation of another language being spoken. The group leaders, who were paid minimum wages to talk to interesting foreigners, thought it was great. However, Lund was very selective: through an interview and group dynamics screening, she ended up with good listeners who asked student-ego-centred questions, confirmed and encouraged participation, and generally gave a sheltered, limited risk situation in which the ELI students could get used to conversation with natives. (See her article for all the excellent details if you want to try this out.)

Teacher-tutor-adviser

Finally, at the Université de Nancy II (CRAPEL), where experimenting with semi-autonomous learning started in 1974, students are questioned by a professor as to their linguistic goals and then advised on how to attain them. The professor meets with them periodically thereafter. The reality that they admit to is that different people want to know a language for different reasons and will benefit more if they can direct their own studies and learn what they want to learn, how they want to learn it (for various programme descriptions see Holec, 1979 and Dickinson, 1987).

7 Questions of time and position

We've already talked about how we can use the student's interests. We can also allow them more speaking time and organise the placement of furniture to encourage interaction.

Speaking time

A teacher can see to what extent he or she is collaborating with students by recording a lesson and asking the following questions:

a How much do I speak and how much do the students speak? Is the time shared? Do I monopolise the floor? Do I interrupt? Are the students allowed to interrupt me?

b Do I use strategies of unequal encounters and my authority too blatantly, stifling student participation?

c What kinds of things do I say and what kinds of things do the students say? How many questions are from students and how many are from me?

Position

We can also ask ourselves, what is my position in the class? Must the teacher always be standing and in front of the class? Could the tables be arranged in a circle or square, a V or a horseshoe? Can I sit with the students as an equal? Could I stoop or squat down to students (especially young children) when talking to them individually and thus having more eye contact?

Experiment yourself and try to be aware of what the different reactions are from your students. See Dörnyei and Gajdàtsy (1989) for an excellent description of ways to develop quality group dynamics in a student-centred approach.

8 Conference centred writing (CCW)
A one to one classroom composition approach

CCW originated with Roger Garrison, a Los Angeles community college composition teacher in the early 1970s. He decided that having students writing nearly all the time encouraged by short conferences with the teacher was the key to learning to write.

This approach . . . was based on the premises that individuals (not groups) have writing problems, that writing is a skill that can be acquired through practice, that writing teachers should be editors-on-the-spot, that the **quality of time with an instructor was more important than the quantity**, and that self-paced, self-managed learning was real learning. (Sokmen, 1988, my highlighting)

CCW sees students as individuals with individual problems that are more efficiently handled 1/1. The teacher circulates, asking questions that make students discover their own processes of writing. As most composition teachers experience, the diversity of problems and levels in any one class makes teaching general skills to the whole group a difficult task.

CCW's similarity to the 1/1 lessons already outlined is evident. Quality interaction occurs in CCW situations in which the teacher can be intensely relevant to each student's writing needs (avoiding possibly irrelevant mass-mediated discourse), to their psychological and emotional needs, and to their actual composition as it is being written. It emphasises helping someone with the process of learning, rather than dictating norms and then simply judging the product. This classroom application of CCW teaching has been researched and confirmed as efficient in two native speaker environments. Sokmen's (1988) informal observation in ESL settings is that students write better and with more confidence using CCW: 'The quantity of writing seems to affect progress: grammar improves without focus on errors, and being a coach is better than being a red-pen authority. ... That all this is possible without adding to the instructor's preparation time and paper load is remarkable.'

Knowingly or unknowingly, CCW may make writing easier because it also follows a more natural line of development from what we think, through our treatment of it in discussion, and finally in writing. Jumping straight from what we are thinking to writing deprives us of doing a rough draft of our ideas and arguments conversationally. Discussion allows for a first external draft and its adjustment to other interlocutors, their feedback and (non) comprehension being important elements to eventually render our ideas more reader-based. Interpersonal verbal interaction is a poorly understood, but immensely beneficial, first step in the composing process.

9 Examples and sources of 1/1 class materials

In this section I want to present some materials that help teachers to make their classes more interactive. They are examples of ideas and things to look for in the TEFL/TESL market as publishers realise the interest stimulated by research and practice.

Threshold, by Ferguson, O'Reilly and Stojan, was first printed in 1978 by the Center for the Experimentation and Evaluation of Language Learning Techniques in Geneva. Their basic assumptions are that students learn more when there is activity and they are free from tension. They state,

'The whole course is based on three points:

1 students must have a chance to speak in order to learn to speak, to write in order to learn to write
2 if only one person speaks at a time, learning is slow
3 the teacher is an initiator, motivator and coordinator, but not number one performer.'

Therefore their course is organised around students working in pairs in a large class and the teacher circulating to act as a general organiser and adviser. Working in pairs, each person is much more active than with teacher-fronted classes and they also are less tense. Tension is also reduced by having a variety of activities and by asking students to do only what they are capable of doing.

Watcyn-Jones' *Functional English: Pair Work* printed originally in 1981 and reprinted nearly every year since has gained great popularity with language teachers because of its easy to use format. There are two booklets, A and B, for a pair of students. They work on the same activity at the same time but each has different information in their respective books so that they actually need each other to complete the tasks. He explains his reasoning thus:

In most language learning situations there is always an element of the unexpected – of not knowing exactly what the person you are talking to is going to say. . . . Unfortunately, most books give little practice in this since all too often every student has access to the same material as everyone else in the class with the result that anything that is said is often predictable.

Pair Work also trains students to really listen to each other, to ask for clarification, to reformulate, to adjust to each other in order to provide comprehensible input.

Donn Byrne's *Techniques for Classroom Interaction* (1987) describes how interaction can be implemented with whole groups, small groups, and pairs in accuracy and fluency exercises. He provides concrete examples and clear models. He encourages teachers to act like normal human beings when doing fluency exercises and stresses their uniqueness over other material (books, video, tape players) – teachers can interact, they can adjust! And that shows students how to do the same. Only people can adjust to each other. Frozen materials can't respond to a student's multiple forms of feedback; human beings do have this amazing ability. See also Rivers' *Interactive Language Teaching* (1987) which provides more theoretical background and a wide array of ways to get students to use the language interactively.

Postscript

A leading chameleon

As I was practically finished with the seventh draft of the book you're holding, I happened to see Woody Allen's movie *Zellig*. Several parallels with language teaching came to mind. For those of you familiar with the film, you know that it deals comically with the particular supernatural ability of a man who, like a chameleon, is able to become just like the people that he is with. When with a Chinese man, Zellig becomes Chinese, with a fat person he becomes fat, and with the female psychiatrist who is trying to treat him he talks 'psychiatry' and thinks that he is a psychiatrist as he tries to help her. His case is explained as the result of an enormous need to fit in and belong to a group, to be accepted by those closest to him. When he is cured, he at first goes to the opposite extreme of disagreeing with everyone in order to be himself but then later reaches a sort of equilibrium.

In the field of Neuro Linguistic Programming, Bandler and Grinder (1979) describe the ability of gifted therapists to join their client's reality, to act as chameleons, emotionally, linguistically, physically, and psychically. In everyday language we call this 'empathising', and such people are labelled 'charming', but we rarely carry it to the point of mirroring the person completely as Zellig does. Therapists, once having joined their client's reality, are then in rapport and communication flows much more easily. At this point they are able to 'lead' patients in directions that they feel they need to go in order to be more healthy or to overcome problems. Thus their original 'Zelligness' has an ulterior motive. However, this rapport building also depends a great deal on genuinely communicating respect for the other person.

For a teacher, this ability to join the reality of a client/student also builds rapport ('Whatever the children want to communicate about, whatever they want to read about, is our subject matter.' Rivers 1976). With rapport they are more open to learning. The teacher is not imposing her reality on the student, but rather joining the student's in order to make the new language relevant to their reality. **The amount of learning appears to be proportional to the amount of reality-sharing which is dependent upon, and a producer of rapport**. Schematically, the teacher starts as a chameleon but then hopes to give a chameleon ability to the students, allowing them to change from speakers of just their native language into speakers of another language. This doesn't mean that the teacher loses her personality, however. Ideally the teacher is a good communicator who knows how to achieve rapport and get students to mirror her as she mirrors them. But she is also someone who has her own thoughts and opinions and can teach assertiveness, diplomacy, and critical thought at the same time – all dimensions of a good communicator in my opinion. (See Richardson's book *The Magic of Rapport*, 1987.)

Knowing how to adjust to the realities of different people remains in my mind the most important ability of a good communicator. If you can adjust appropriately, rapport and comprehensible input are the result. This adjustment is not only linguistic but deals with the whole person and communication in its many facets. 'Your words without your soul are meaningless. Your eyes without your passion are empty. A teacher is no teacher, a mother no mother, who feeds children meaningless emptiness.' (Tanak Akay, my grandma, c. 1900)

She also wrote: 'Does the grower cultivate a field and plant seeds? Or, is it the earth that cultivates the grower and plants ideas? The sky cannot water the earth without first taking a drink from her. You see, the earth feasts on the best of us, making us bountiful. Give and take, my child. Neither alone suffices.'

May Zellig and Grandma be with you. It's been nice talking to you.

Glossary

affective inhibition/affective filter

these terms normally refer to the effect that feelings can have on learning. If we feel attacked, insecure, frightened, or frustrated we are not open to learning and spend our energy protecting ourselves. (see Krashen 1981)

concrete referents

these are things one can see and possibly touch in the here and now as opposed to abstract ideas which require one to create a context mentally only from the symbolic value of words.

CIWA

the name of a 1/1 language service in Geneva, Switzerland, in which a central office finds teachers willing to go to the student's home or business (p. 36)

EFL

English as a Foreign Language (see ESL)

ESL

English as a Second Language. ESL includes EFL in some writers' uses. For most teachers in countries where English is not a native language, ESL is teaching English within an English speaking country and EFL is teaching it elsewhere. Some say the distinction is irrelevant. Others assert that the language experience outside the classroom changes all. These last also sometimes complain that most materials and theory in the profession is ESL oriented and poorly suited to EFL. As one would expect, definitions and arguments change according to where you are and what you experience.

ETAS

English Teachers Association Switzerland

IATEFL

International Association of Teachers of English as a Foreign Language, originating in England in 1967.

TEFL/TESL

Teaching EFL or ESL

TESOL

Teachers of English to Speakers of Other Languages, the international association of teachers of ESL and EFL originating in the USA in 1966.

unequal encounter

when one person in a situation has power over the other(s), typically police, judges, doctors, and lawyers. But anyone who has a certain knowledge that is being esteemed may have the possibility of being the superior person in the encounter. Equalising the encounter usually creates more interaction and less dictating. (See Thomas 1984.)

References

Abraham, H 1983 *Skiing Right* Harper and Row, San Francisco

Alber, J L et Py, B 1985 Vers un modèle de la communication interculturelle: interparole, coopération, et conversation. *Etudes de linguistique appliquée* 61:78–90

Allwright, D 1984a The importance of interaction in classroom language learning *Applied Linguistics* 5(2):156–71

Allwright, D 1984b Why don't learners learn what teachers teach? – the interaction hypothesis. Language learning in formal and informal contexts. Proceedings of a joint seminar of the Irish and British Associations for Applied Linguistics 11–13 September pp. 3–18

Allwright, D 1986a Classroom observation: problems and possibilities. Paper given at RELC Regional Seminar: Patterns of classroom interaction in Southeast Asia April 21–25

Allwright, D 1986b Making sense of instruction: What's the problem? In *Papers in Applied Linguistics-Michigan* (PALM) 1(2):1–11 Winter

Allwright, R L 1982 Perceiving and pursuing learners' needs. In Geddes, M and Sturtridge, G (eds.) *Individualism* Modern English Publications: 24–31

Asher, J 1977 *Learning Another Language Through Actions: The Complete Teacher's Guide* Sky Oak Publications, Los Gatos, California

August, D 1987 Effects of peer tutoring on the second language acquisition of Mexican American children in elementary school *TESOL Quarterly* 21(4):717–36

Bandler, R and Grinder, J 1979 *Frogs into Princes* Real People Press, Moab, Utah

Barber, E J W 1980 Language acquisition and applied linguistics *ADFL Bulletin* 12:26–32

Bassano, S and Christison, M A 1988 Cooperative learning in the ESL classroom *TESOL Newsletter* 22(2)

de Beaugrande, R and Dressler, W 1981 *Introduction to Text Linguistics* Longman

Bejarano, Y 1987 A cooperative small-group methodology in the language classroom *TESOL Quarterly* 21(3):483–504

Berne, E 1964 *Games People Play* Ballantine Books, New York

Blagden, J 1988 A Teacher as a Student *English Teachers Association Switzerland, Newsletter* 5(2):11–13

Bornoz, P 1988 Avatars of a tradition: a survey of five Victorian fairy tales Unpublished M.A. mémoire, Université de Neuchâtel, Switzerland

Bowen, D and Madsen, H 1978 *Adaptation in Language Teaching* Newbury House, Rowley MA

Bronckart, J-P 1987 Interactions, discours, significations *Langue Française* 67:29–50

Brown, R 1977 Introduction in Snow, C and Ferguson, C (eds.) *Talking to Children* Cambridge University Press

Byrne, D 1987 *Techniques for Classroom Interaction* Longman

Cohen, A 1984 Introspecting about second language learning. Paper presented at the 9th ILASH Conference, Netanya, Israel

Curran, C 1976 *Counseling-Learning in Second Languages* Apple River Press

Dainty, P 1986 *Marilyn Monroe* Collins

Dickens, C 1837 *The Posthumous Papers of The Pickwick Club*

Dickinson, L 1987 *Self-instruction in Language Learning* Cambridge University Press

Dingwall, S (ed.) 1988 *Legally Lost? Brief information for English teachers working in Switzerland* ETAS publication no 2 (Available from editor, Sternstr 7, 5417 Nussbaumen, Switzerland)

Doise, W, Rijsman, J, Van Meel, J, Bressers, I and Pinxten, W 1981 Sociale marketing en cognitieve ontwikkeling *Pedgogisch Studien* 58:241–48

Dörnyei, Z and Gajdàtsy, K 1989 A student-centred approach to language teaching 1 and 2 *Practical English Teaching* March and June

Duda, R 1985 Apprendre à apprendre les langues: 'mais je veux être un handicapé linguistique!' *TRANEL* 8:7–16

Durban, C 1988 Latest survey results – EFL working conditions in France *TESOL France News* Summer

Ferguson, N, O'Reilly, M and Stojan, J 1978 *Threshold* CEEL (Center for the experimentation and evaluation of language learning techniques), Geneva

Freudenstein, R (ed.) 1981 *Language Incorporated* Pergamon/Hueber, Oxford/ Munich

Gallwey, W T 1974 *The Inner Game of Tennis* Bantam Books, Toronto

Gardner, R C and Lambert, W E 1972 *Attitudes and Motivation in Second Language Learning* Newbury House, Rowley, MA

Garrison, R 1974 One-to-one: tutorial instruction in freshman composition *New Directions for Community College* 2(1):55–83

Hatch, E 1978 *Second Language Acquisition* Newbury House, Rowley, MA

Holec, H 1979 *Autonomy and Foreign Language Learning* Pergamon Press

Hutchinson, T and Waters, A 1986 *English for Specific Purposes, a learning-centred approach* Cambridge University Press

Klippel, F 1984 *Keep Talking* Cambridge University Press

Kramsch, C 1985 Interaction processes in group work *TESOL Quarterly* 19(4):796–800

Krashen, S 1981 *Second Language Acquisition and Second Language Learning* Pergamon Press

Krashen, S 1984 *Writing: Research, Theory, and Applications* Pergamon Press

Krashen, S 1985 *The Input Hypothesis: issues and implications* Longman

Krashen, S and Terrell, T 1983 *The Natural Approach* Pergamon Press

Light, P and Perret-Clermont, A N 1986 Social construction of logical structures or social construction of meaning? *Dossiers de psychology* 27 Université de Neuchâtel

Long, M 1983 Linguistic and conversational adjustments to non-native speakers *Studies in Second Language Acquisition* 5(2):177–94

Long, M 1985 Input and second language acquisition theory. In Gass, S and Madden, C (eds.) *Input in Second Language Acquisition* (pp. 377–93) Newbury House, Rowley, MA

Lund, J 1981 Creating conversation groups *Gulf TESOL Newsletter* 1(4):8–13

McPherson, K 1987 One to one teaching: a person-centred approach *Modern English Teacher* 14(3):41–3

Moskowitz, G 1978 *Caring and Sharing in the Foreign Language Class* Newbury House, Rowley, MA

Murphey, T 1979 Situationally motivated teacher produced texts Unpublished M.A. thesis, University of Florida

Murphey, T 1985a World Englishes: raison d'être of situationally motivated teacher produced texts *TESOL Newsletter*, June

Murphey, T 1985b ESP for youth: teaching for peak relevance using international pop music *TESOL Newsletter*, December

Murphey, T 1989 The when where and who of pop lyrics: the listener's prerogative. *Pop Music* 8(2):58–70

Murphey, T 1990a *Music and song in language learning: an analysis of pop song lyrics and the use of music and song in TEFL* (PhD dissertation, Université de Neuchâtel, Switzerland) Peter Lang Verlag, Bern, Switzerland

Murphey, T 1990b The song stuck in my head phenomena: the melodic din in the LAD? *System* 18(1):53–64

Naisbitt, J 1982 *Megatrends: Ten New Directions Transforming Our Lives* Warner Books, New York

Parr, PC and Krashen, S 1986 Involuntary rehearsal of second language in beginning and advanced performers *System* 14:275–278

Peck, A 1988 *Language Teachers at Work* Prentice Hall, New York

Perret-Clermont, A N, and Mugny, G 1985 En guise de conclusion: effets sociologiques et processus didactiques. In Mugny, G *Psychologie sociale du développement cognitif*, Coll exploration, Berne

Pica, T, Young, R and Doughty, C 1987 The impact of interaction on comprehension *TESOL Quarterly* 21(4):737–58

Porter Ladousse, G 1983 *Speaking Personally* Cambridge University Press

Redfield, M 1986 The M.A. and TEFL *TESOL Newsletter* 20(6):15

Richardson, J 1987 *The Magic of Rapport* Meta Publications, Cupertino, California

Rivers, W M 1976 *Speaking in Many Tongues: Essays in Foreign Language Teaching* Newbury House, Rowley, MA

Rivers, W M 1987 *Interactive Language Teaching* Cambridge University Press

Rotzoll, K B 1985 Advertisements. In van Dijk, T A (ed.) *Discourse and Communication, New Approaches to the Analyses of Mass Media Discourse and Communication* de Gruyter, Berlin: 94–105

Sacks, O 1985 *The Man Who Mistook His Wife for a Hat* Pan Books

Scarlin, W and Eliason, D 1986 Baden/Brugg Branch Report of the *English Teachers Association Switzerland Newsletter* 3(4):8–9

Schoener, W 1986 The third world student as teacher *TESOL Newsletter* 20(6):9

Simon, S B, Howe, L W and Kirschenbaum, H 1972 *Values Clarification: a handbook of practical strategies for teachers and students* Dodd, Mead and Company, New York

Sinclair, J McH and Brazil, D 1982 *Teacher Talk* Oxford University Press

Sokmen, A 1988 Taking advantage of conference-centered writing *TESOL Newsletter* 22(1):1, February

Sperber, D and Wilson D 1986 *Relevance: Communication and Cognition* Basil Blackwell

Stevick, E 1971 *Adapting and Writing Language Lessons* U.S. Department of State (distributed by TESOL)

Stevick, E 1976 *Memory, Meaning and Method: some psychological perspectives on language learning* Newbury House, Rowley, MA

Stevick, E 1980 *Teaching Languages: A Way and Ways* Newbury House, Rowley, MA

Strong, M 1983 Social styles and the second language acquisition of Spanish-speaking kindergartners *TESOL Quarterly* 17:241–58

Thomas, J 1984 Cross-cultural discourse as 'unequal-encounter': towards a pragmatic analysis. *Applied Linguistics* 5(3):226–35

Underhill, A 1988 Teaching without a coursebook *English Teachers Association Switzerland Newsletter* 5(1):12–13

Varonis, E and Gass, S 1985 Non-native/non-native conversations: a model for negotiation of meaning *Applied Linguistics* 6(1)

Vygotsky, L 1934/1962 *Thought and Language* MIT Press

Watcyn-Jones, P 1986 *Functional English: Pair Work* (Student books A and B) Penguin Books, New York

Wilberg, P 1987 *One to One* Sussex Language Teaching Publications

Wordell, C (ed.) 1985 *A Guide to Teaching English in Japan* The Japan Times

Wright, A 1987 *How to Communicate Successfully* Cambridge University Press

Further reading

The newsletters of the learner independence special interest group of IATEFL
(International Association of Teachers of English as a Foreign Language)

Dawe, C W and Dornan, E A 1984 *One to One: resources for conference centred writing* (second edition) Little, Brown and Company, Boston

English for Specific Purposes (formerly the ESP Journal) Pergamon Press

Frank, C and Rinvolucri, M 1983 *Grammar in Action* Pergamon, Oxford and Hueber, Munich

Gaies, S J 1985 *Peer Involvement in Language Learning* Prentice Hall Regents, Englewood Cliffs

Gass, S and Madden, C 1985 *Input in Second Language Acquisition*, Newbury House, Cambridge, MA

Gass, S and Varonis, E 1984 The effect of familiarity on the comprehensibility of non-native speech *Language Learning* 34(1):65–88

Grosjean, F 1985 The bilingual as a competent but specific speaker-hearer *Journal of Multilingual and Multicultural Development* 6(6)467–77

Jones, L 1984 *Ideas* Cambridge University Press

Long, M 1983 Native speaker/non-native speaker conversation and the negotiation of comprehensible input *Applied Linguistics* 4(2)

Long, M and Porter, P 1985 Group work, interlanguage talk, and second language acquisition *TESOL Quarterly* 19(2)

Murphey, T 1986 De la coopération à l'ajustement collaboratif polylogal dans les cours de langue *TRANEL 11* Institut de Linguistique, Université de Neuchâtel

Murphey, T 1988 'When will we see us again?' Variety minorization and restructuration in allovariety contact (in press): *Actes du Symposium "Minorisation et interaction"* Droz, Geneva

Py, B 1986 Making sense: interlanguage's intertalk in exolingual conversation *Studies in Second Language Acquisition* 8:343–53

Ramsey, G 1987 *Images* Longman

Rinvolucri, M 1984 *Grammar Games* Cambridge University Press

Spaventa, L (ed.) 1980 *Towards the Creative Teaching of English* George Allen and Unwin

Waltz, J 1986 Increasing student-talk time in the foreign language classroom *The Canadian Modern Language Review* 425:952–67

Appendix I

1/1 Teacher discussion group: Handout 1

The following is a list of disadvantages that 1/1 teachers listed concerning their teaching situations. Which would you agree with? With a partner try to decide 1) if you think it is really a disadvantage, 2) how serious it is, and 3) how it might be overcome. Finally, are some of these problems not particular to 1/1 but to all teaching? Try to use concrete examples as much as possible in your arguments.

Student disadvantages

- no other students to get ideas from, and to work and converse with
- no other students to compare self with
- pressure of performance – no slack time
- no chance to rest and digest
- class fixed on one person – hears only teacher's English
- doesn't feel among equals
- no group activities, can't practise third person singular
- teacher may advance too quickly
- very tiring
- difficult to get out of arrangement – can't just drop out
- can be expensive

Teacher disadvantages

- preparation of materials, meeting student's needs, maintaining enthusiasm
- very concentrated work for teacher, no interaction between students, consequently no 'breathing time' for teacher
- loss of overall view of language problems due to one-to-one situation
- time consuming preparation
- no possibility for games, rather dry
- boring, lacks stimulus of large class, less demanding
- last minute cancellation, irregularity
- if student is not responsive, teacher is probably too verbal
- teacher often does not charge full rate as she feels sorry for the poor student
- teacher has to adapt to one student's learning style and (possibly even) whims; may get boring or frightening if student is difficult and/or has trouble relating to other people; teacher may feel obliged to please one person (servant role)

Appendix 2

1/1 Teacher discussion group: Handout 2

To discuss:
How are teachers similar to police, doctors, politicians, scientists, preachers, and farmers? Which one would you choose to represent metaphorically your idea of what a teacher should be? Can you think of any other professions that could be compared with that of a teacher? How do you feel when you are driving and you see a policeman just behind you? How do you feel when you have a conference with your doctor or lawyer? How do you feel when you talk to someone that you feel is your equal but for whom you have a lot of respect? How do think your students feel when they talk to you? If they compared your teaching with another role, profession, or position which one or two would they choose?

In *Saturday Night*, September 1987
From Marshall McLuhan to Pierre Trudeau
June 13, 1974.
Dear Pierre:
May I venture to suggest an approach to the women's lib matter? Women are less specialised than men, and long accustomed to adapting to a variety of roles. In our new instant information environment, most men who have been accustomed to specialist jobs and functions must now switch from role to role in the course of a day. In the big hierarchies this creates extreme discomfort and dismay and it is increasingly obvious that women could perform many of these functions better than men.

Do you agree with the above analysis? What roles are called into play when teaching 1/1? Which are problems for you and how do you handle them?

Appendix 3

1/1 Teacher discussion group: Handout 3

Below are some observations concerning 1/1 and teaching and learning in general. Discuss them with a partner and see if you agree or disagree with them; try to provide a personal example to support your opinion.

■ Observation 1
Your students are your best publicity.

■ Observation 2
If possible make English the only language of communication from the very beginning and it becomes the accepted standard.

■ Observation 3
The efficient learner has the practised ability to change mass media

discourse into personally relevant communication, to imagine that the speaker or writer is addressing her.

■ Observation 4

Having *instrumental* motivation means learning things that one sees as useful for life, and it not only makes learning more interesting but more efficient. With learning that is merely *incidental*, the goals are generally getting on with things and getting good grades, not actually using the language. A third kind of motivation, and the most efficient in some people's opinion, is *integrative*, in which the student identifies with the group, or wants to become part of the group, that speaks the language.

■ Observation 5

Agreeing (or suggesting) to meet with no obligation to discuss possible lessons gives more control to the student. Clients may be more apt to consider teachers who don't give them a hard sell. It's a start of equal encounters.

■ Observation 6

The flexibility of the teacher is of great importance as far as meeting place and time.

■ Observation 7

Often the clients still need something to make them feel your meetings are somewhat like school. Even if they are progressing a lot, the enjoyment and naturalness may make them doubt the efficiency of the method because they learned in school that studying is supposed to be more difficult.

■ Observation 8

The pain of error correction can, however, be avoided, e.g. by taking notes and only interrupting if the communication breaks down (i.e. you don't understand).

■ Observation 9

When the teacher generates an intense and genuine interest in the client and the client's interests, feeling sincerely that the client has as much to teach as to learn, the creation of an *equal encounter* situation is easier.

■ Observation 10

A teacher may plan extensively and have a stock of topics to discuss and materials to exploit, but does not need to feel tied to them.

■ Observation 11

The private teacher can become a valuable language acquisition consultant, advising the student first on ways to improve and speed up language learning, and secondly on ways to shape the language learning environment for increased contact time.

■ Observation 12

In order to attain an approximate level of 'equal encounter' a student learning a language can offer something of value to her partners.

Observation 13
Part of a teacher's adjusting seems to be figuring out to what extent the student wants lessons resembling school or simply social contact. The tenet of conventional education is that school is most efficient, but experience does not always show this to be true. What seems true is that individual students will learn more if they're convinced they are doing what they think is best, they are in control, and they are enjoying it (these are not necessarily mutually compatible criteria).

Observation 14
The language teacher in a classroom may dominate too much when always proceeding in a lecture fashion, rather than stimulating the students to interact and use the language while the teacher is in the background. This same danger may exist in 1/1 teaching if teachers merely use the lessons as time to talk to a captive audience.

Observation 15
Using a language internationally between non-natives may have an equal encounter effect that is healthy. Neither participant has the advantage of merely speaking their native language, but rather both must adjust with humility and pay more attention to their partner.

Observation 16
Adjusting to your student's enthusiasm and interests may necessitate a readjustment of your own priorities at a given moment in your life, or at least an acceptance of their interests without derogatory judgement.

Observation 17
Although the traditionally professed goal for language teachers is student progress, for certain students at certain levels, maintenance and 'keeping the batteries charged' may be their primary reason for taking lessons. Social contact may be primary for still others. However, learning new things is still very much a part of the process, for the 'recharging' is best done when going somewhere, and social contact most interesting when doing challenging things with the language. The emphasis here is principally on using and keeping useful the muscles that are already there.

Observation 18
Corresponding with students and sending them cards, notes, and articles relevant to their interests is very positive and good publicity. Not only do they feel that the teacher's concern for them goes beyond the hour lesson (which it should), but they in turn are on the lookout for the teacher's good too: sending articles of interest and more students. Correspondence is another element adding to the equal encounter.

Observation 19
Perhaps the single greatest service that I provide to many executives is simply one of added *confidence* that they can express themselves, that they

can get their messages across, that they need have no feelings of inadequacy when attempting to express themselves. I am providing a 'sheltered' situation where they can risk themselves with limited liability – I am not really a customer. I am also an encouraging listener and avid questioner so that their concentration is more on the message than the form.

■ Observation 20

Students should be encouraged to select materials themselves although this is traditionally the teacher's role, as they will usually be more motivated when they have the choice. However, the teacher needs to be sensitive enough to see when perhaps they are too difficult and advise the student to change.

■ Observation 21

Perhaps one of the ways to avoid frustration as a teacher is to recognise the students' need for social contact as well as their professed need to do serious work.

■ Observation 22

Some students are good communicators in that they can feign understanding thus encouraging more input from the people they meet. However, they can sometimes do this too much and fan the flame of talk coming from a loquacious teacher.

■ Observation 23

Students dropping the 1/1 meetings after a while should not necessarily be taken as a sign that something was wrong with a teacher or her way of teaching. The good thing about most 1/1 is that it is ecologically self regulating: if, for either of the parties, meetings become unwanted, for whatever reason, they can be discontinued – a very healthy option not available in public schools.

■ Observation 24

An exchange of money for services rendered defines the meetings as valuable exchanges. Without it, lessons risk falling into rather artificial meetings between friends which may ultimately become uncomfortable for both parties because one doesn't know if they are professional or merely social.

■ Observation 25

In 1/1 language teaching, the personality of the teacher is very important. Learning EFL methodology, although generally providing useful tools, may lead to artificial 'teacherese' rather than the naturally efficient interaction many untrained teachers are already capable of. The ideal teacher is of course a highly trained teacher who also remains empathetic and broadminded. However, the trained teacher runs the danger of turning her potentially rich encounters into abstract 'classes'. Interaction with communicators who adjust well seems to be the most fertile ground for acquisition. Training can help, but may also get in the way at times.

Doing things with the target language may intensify the learning experience and make it easier because of the natural concrete referents offered by the situations (as opposed to the abstractions too often offered in 'sit and imagine' classes).

Appendix 4

1/1 Teacher discussion group: Handout 4
Statements for discussion

What does each of the statements below mean for you? Do you agree or disagree? How might you change or qualify the statement in order to make it acceptable? In each case try to give concrete examples to back up your opinions. (in pairs)

1 One doesn't teach a language, one teaches a student.

2 Teachers have a lot to learn from students.

3 Learning is best done in school.

4 In school, good marks replace learning as the principal goal.

5 Authority, not respect, is the predominant controlling force for most teachers.

6 The teacher is the most valuable element in a lesson.

7 Without proper books and materials, language study is extremely poor.

8 Teachers know the best way for a person to learn a language.

9 Learners only learn mistakes from each other.

10 A turtle trying to fly is more admirable than a bird sitting in a tree.

Appendix 5

Conversation Exchange form (see page 107)

THE CONVERSATION EXCHANGE

Do you need conversation practice in English or another language?

The conversation exchange programme puts students together who wish to practise conversing in each other's language. Usually you meet over lunch or a cup of coffee and speak your native language half the time and the other person's language half the time, in a friendly, helpful environment. You and your partner are completely free to arrange where, how, and how long you meet, or to stop meeting. All the coordinator does is give you each other's form. It worked well for over 50 people last year. **Try it!**

Name _____ Native language(s) _____

Other languages spoken fluently _____

Desired language(s) to practice _____

Telephone _____

Address _____

Age _____ Sex _____

Academic interests _____

Sports _____

Hobbies _____

A favourite proverb or saying _____

Please return all forms to: Tim Murphey
English Seminar (E 48) Comtesse 2, 2000 Neuchâtel.

(on the back of the conversation exchange form)

> Hi!
> When you receive your partner's form please contact them as soon as possible to arrange your first meeting at a place you both know and at a convenient time. Describe yourself and what you will be wearing. The first meeting may be a bit difficult, use the information on these forms to ask questions about each other and to stimulate conversation. Good Luck.
>
> P.S. If you would like another partner, or two partners, come by the English Seminar and see me. Or if you have any questions, please call 21 31 81.

Conversational topics if you need them (to ask your partner about).
Describe:

your family
your apartment
your ideal job
your country
your best friend(s)
your favourite meals
your favourite films (actors/actresses)
your favourite books
your favourite music, songs, singers
your favourite vacations
your ideal job

What is on your agenda for the next week?
What have you done this past week? Today, so far?

Why do you want to practise another language?
What do you like about speaking another language?
How do you think one learns a language best?

cities
nature
sports
T.V.
radio
newspapers

Appendix 6

Exchange rates as of December 1990

(This exchange rate table accompanies the discussion concerning fees in Chapter 5.)

Swiss approximate rates for 1/1 lessons (as of 1989)
Beginning rate, student-teachers   SFrs 20
small town professional   30–40
large city professional   40–60
in a language school   50–90

Approximate monetary exchange rates as of December 1990

Swiss Franc	U.S. Dollar	Jap. Yen	G.B. £	FF	GMark	Lire (100 units)	Saudi Arabia
10	7.90	1050	3.80	40	9	95	30
20	15.80	2100	7.40	80	18	190	60
30	23.70	3150	11.20	120	27	285	90
40	31.60	4200	15.00	160	36	380	120
50	39.50	5250	18.80	200	45	475	150
60	47.40	6300	22.60	240	54	570	180
70	55.30	7350	26.40	280	63	665	210
80	63.20	8400	30.20	320	72	760	240
90	71.10	9450	34.00	360	81	855	270
100	79.00	10000	37.80	400	90	950	300

Appendix 7

Parable on eclecticism
On the expressway of life: Applications to teaching ESOL

A man started out in a wagon. He felt he knew where he was going, he was confident, and his wagon rolled well for him. Others saw him and his contented face. He even went so far as to write books about how he had found contentment.

Some of the people began jumping up and down screaming, 'Look, he has found the meaning of life! He has all the answers.' And so they all (well, at least many) jumped on the wagon. The band and all.

The poor man was at first pleased, then troubled. He knew the wagon worked for him but that others would not at all be content rolling where he was going. But for a while they all smiled as children do at the end of a fairy tale, happy-ever-after.

But after happy-ever-after, some became upset. They thought the man should go faster or slower, in one direction or another. And he did not control the weather at all! They got off the wagon and joined another going the other way, saying they had tried and his wagon was doomed. Soon even half the band joined the other wagon, provoking a cacophony of discordant melodies.

The poor man was upset. But luckily he saw his direction was still true for him, although he admitted it might not be for everyone. For some he saw it rolled pleasantly enough but usually only some of the time. He finally stopped his wagon and sat beside the expressway of life and thought and thought. He read a little bit, too.

Finally he said, 'I think it's best if people find their own wagons and are responsible for their own direction. Then they can travel roads that are suited to them and construct their wagons the way they like.'

The people didn't care much for his advice. They preferred fairy tales and band wagons. They were more secure in letting others decide what to do and then blaming them if it didn't work. But some smiled a knowing smile. And the world turned.

Sometimes methodologies are something like religions – they work because people believe in them. So perhaps the important thing is to believe in what you do, or to find something worth believing in. But it is nice (and practical) to be open to the beauties in all religions (methods) and to avoid confining yourself to any one dogma (pseudo fairy tale god) simply because you 'chose' it. Investing ourselves in one direction sometimes makes it difficult to see the value in other directions.

We have evolved beyond the binary idea of 'choose one and call the rest sacrilege'. Eclecticism proudly and paradoxically states that 'it's true and so is the contrary', for it realises the realities of individual adjustment and selection to unique situations.

Amen (though I be damned by the band).
Tim Murphey
(originally printed in *TESOL Newsletter* 4/85)

Appendix 8

Insearch

I recently found a new way to describe the process of using the student and her information as the primary resource for my language teaching. I call the process *insearch* and contrast it with *input*.

I'm doing insearch when I ask students to search for information that they already have and to give that to me so that I might use it more fully in interaction. For example, I might ask adolescents what their favourite songs and artists are and why they like them. I might ask a teachers' group to think of a teacher who had a big impression on them while students and to describe the important qualities. This would be contrasted with deciding myself what songs I think students like or what qualities a good teacher has and then feeding this to my classes – this is input without concern for quality interaction and with little respect for the schemata of information already present.

The power of insearch stems from several of its inherent characteristics.

1 I am immediately in interaction with the group that I am dealing with, not doing something to the group.
2 There is a natural information gap on both sides which helps establish a more equal encounter.
3 Group members feel more valued because their opinions and information stocks are being used and respected as in natural communication.
4 All the above increase motivation because of the possibility to clarify, explain, and negotiate 'meaning' which is not known beforehand.
5 It cuts down on high-risk teacher guess-work concerning relevant materials and information selection.
6 It cuts down on teacher preparation time since the insearched material of each participant is a type of self-input for themselves and for the others in the group. Information that is gathered in an insearch situation can be further exploited in later classes. For example, in composition classes I ask students to write down what they think the qualities of a good essay are and the process they use for writing one. For the next class, I have typed all of these out on a handout and I ask them to discuss them in small groups, deciding which they feel are valid and which ones invalid.
7 Doing insearch allows students to learn from each other, realising that there are many ways to think and do things. It creates a more 'team' atmosphere where one is more willing to participate, challenge, and risk.
8 Insearch allows teachers to adjust their teaching to the levels and interests of the students, to their known stock of knowledge, not to teach things that they already show they know, and not to teach things that are too far beyond them. ·
9 It's fun! In short, it allows for the production of well adjusted comprehensible input through quality interaction.

Appendix 9

ALF (Alternative Learning Forms)/A 1/1 business run by university students

As last drafts of this book are being reviewed, I am busily finishing a research project in Switzerland before going to Japan for a new position.

The research project's original goal was to establish a service inside the Université de Neuchâtel in which trained students would give 1/1 lessons to clients in the private sector. In November of 1989 I gave a six hour introductory training course to 31 interested university students. I then distributed their names and phone numbers to businesses and interested parties. Very little happened. The ones who did find work found it most often through me, as I contacted businesses and administrators in person. It became clear to me that the service needed a more entrepreneurial structure.

It also became apparent to me that when I left the university the idea would probably die, since a university's bureaucracy reacts slowly and is not very client-commercially oriented. I then had the idea of forming a junior company run by the students for themselves. I found two enthusiastic students who had taken my introductory course to run the business: one, doing a business degree, to act as the 'manager' and another, studying linguistics, to act as the 'teaching resource coordinator'. Thus, in addition to finding work for students it also is a real experience for students who wish to run a company. For those who teach, it gives practical experience while they study and some money to help them support themselves.

The company calls itself ALF (Alternative Learning Forms) and its principal product is 1/1 lessons. However, it is open to adjust to the needs and wants of the market (e.g. translations, telephone exercises, and individualised cassettes made from a client's curriculum vitae) and thus has as its motto 'Your needs are the inspiration of our creativity'.

ALF's chances of survival are good at this point: there are few costs and there is the possibility of receiving sponsorship from the private sector interested in being known among students, and also some help from the university. Its set up is similar to that of the 1/1 service companies already discussed in Chapter 3. However, Neuchâtel is a small town and it takes time and persistence to introduce new ways of doing things.

The idea could well be implemented by other university students. Students at other universities who wish for more information might try writing to ALF, Université de Neuchâtel, CH–2000 Neuchâtel, Switzerland. (Written January 1990)

Appendix 10

A brief view from Japan

(September 1990, as I am reading over galley proofs of this book)

I've been teaching in Japan about four months as I write this. From what
I can see so far, most of what this book contains also applies to Japan.
But there are a few observations concerning the situation here that might
enlighten others concerning 1/1 teaching and learning. Simply that in
Japan, it is literally everywhere. In fact it seems to be part of the
uninstitutionalised core of Japanese education.

At least half of the native-speaker university professors teach some
private 1/1 lessons. But what is amazing to me is that about 80 per cent of
my students at the university give private lessons to high school students in
some subject. It's an accepted fact that if one wants to get into a good
university, private tutoring and special *juku* schools are a must – public
schooling is simply not enough.

One would think that if 1/1 really worked that all the Japanese high
school students would then be fluent by the time they reached university.
Actually, most university students are still unable to communicate orally in
a foreign language if they haven't been abroad for an extended stay. So
what's the problem? Well the language and culture of Japan *is* very
different. But that's only part of the picture.

Actually, 1/1 teaching does work very well for the goals they have
set. It's just that oral communication is not one of them. Their major
goal is passing the university entrance exams which are based
mostly on rote learning, grammar, reading, and sometimes a bit of
listening – but no productive written or speaking skills. From reading the
unsolicited descriptions of tutoring (that my students write in their English
journals for my classes), I see that they become very involved with their
students. Their attachment for each other tells me that a feeling of rapport
is extremely important for them. Thus 1/1 is efficient, even when the
information is dictated from without, probably due to the bonding and
fine-tuning that comes with individual attention. The 1/1 lessons still have
a strong social element; it's just that it is in Japanese. That my students
write of their tutoring freely also clues me in to the importance that it has
in their agendas and for their finances.

As for oral communication, until it becomes the criterion upon which
universities accept students, most high school students are not going to
feel **the need** to learn how to speak, nor will teachers see the need to
teach toward those ends. 1/1 does work very well, it is simply the Japanese
irony that it is used to ram home mostly information that is used only to get
into universities and then never really operationalised afterwards.

(Thanks to Yuichi Kondo for comments concerning this section.)